Religious Leadership
in National Political Conflicts

Religious Leadership in National Political Conflicts

Bishop Abel Tendekayi Muzorewa and the National Struggle against Colonial Rule in Zimbabwe

LLOYD T. NYAROTA

WIPF & STOCK · Eugene, Oregon

RELIGIOUS LEADERSHIP IN NATIONAL POLITICAL CONFLICTS
Bishop Abel Tendekayi Muzorewa and the National Struggle against Colonial Rule in Zimbabwe

Copyright © 2013 Lloyd T. Nyarota. All rights reserved. Except for brief quotations in critical publications or reviews, no part of this book may be reproduced in any manner without prior written permission from the publisher. Write: Permissions, Wipf and Stock Publishers, 199 W. 8th Ave., Suite 3, Eugene, OR 97401.

Wipf & Stock
An Imprint of Wipf and Stock Publishers
199 W. 8th Ave., Suite 3
Eugene, OR 97401
www.wipfandstock.com

ISBN 13: 978-1-62032-566-7
Manufactured in the U.S.A.

All scripture quotations, unless otherwise indicated, are taken from the Holy Bible, New International Version®, NIV®. Copyright ©1973, 1978, 1984 by Biblica, Inc.™ Used by permission of Zondervan. All rights reserved worldwide.

This book is dedicated to my two children, Lorraine Tinovimba Chiratidzo and Lloyd Tinotenda Nyasha, my late mother, Clara Nyarota, who worked hard to see to it that I received basic education during difficult times, my wife (Mai Tino), my relatives, and my friends, all of whom accorded me both spiritual and moral support during the writing of this book and during the original research for the study of a master's degree.

Contents

Abbreviations ix
Acknowledgments xi
Foreword by Bishop Woodie W. White xiii
Definition of Terms xvii

1 Introduction 1

2 Church Leadership and Political Challenges 4

3 The Political Call 8

4 Church and State 17

5 Toward a Political Career 25

6 The Formation of the United African National Council (1975) 28

7 United African National Council, the Bishop's Own Path 35

8 Internal Settlement or Intensified War: The Bishop Chooses 40

9 Zimbabwe-Rhodesia 51

10 Lancaster House Agreement 60

11 Reflections of People Who Were Involved with Bishop Muzorewa 64

12 Conclusion 79

Epilogue 83
Appendix Interview Questionnaires 85
Bibliography 89

Abbreviations

AACC	All Africa Conference of Churches
ANC	African National Council
ANC-Z	African National Council-Zimbabwe
CCR	Christian Council of Rhodesia
ELCZ	Evangelical Lutheran Church in Zimbabwe
FLS	Front Line States
FROLIZI	Front for the Liberation of Zimbabwe
NDP	National Democratic Party
OAU	Organization of African Union
PCR	Programme to Combat Racism
PF	Patriotic Front
RF	Rhodesia Front
SCM	Student Christian Movement
UANC	United African National Council
UCCZ	United Church of Christ in Zimbabwe
UDI	Unilateral Declaration of Independence
UMC	United Methodist Church
UN	United Nations
USA	United States of America
UTC	United Theological College
WCC	World Council of Churches
ZANU	Zimbabwe African National Unity

Abbreviations

ZANLA	Zimbabwe African National Liberation Army
ZAPU	Zimbabwe African Peoples' Union
ZCC	Zimbabwe Council of Churches
ZIPRA	Zimbabwe People's Revolutionary Army
ZNLWVA	Zimbabwe National Liberation War Veterans Association

Acknowledgments

THIS BOOK WAS DEVELOPED from a master's thesis, and I would like to first and foremost thank my academic supervisor, Reverend Shirley DeWolf, for her support, advice, and encouragement during the research and compilation of the dissertation. She tirelessly responded to my calls for help and directed my attention to any pertinent issues, which I have addressed in this book. She also kept me focused on this project amid numerous assignments.

I wish to extend my deepest gratitude to Mr. Earnest Muzorewa, who kept on encouraging me to write and publish my dissertation in a book form. He believed that the book would fill a big void in the history of Zimbabwe. I am also truly indebted to Rev. Dr. Gwinyai H. Muzorewa, who not only introduced me to theology in seminary but took the pains to edit this book. However, I take responsibility for any errors that may occur in this book. Finally, I give glory to God, who promised never to leave me alone.

Foreword

METHODISM HAS A LONG history of social and political engagement in societal events. Indeed, founder John Wesley and the early Methodist movement played an important role in shaping eighteenth-century England. Wesley was an outspoken anti-slavery advocate and challenged the child labor laws in England as well as the working conditions under which miners labored.

This strong position of social and political advocacy followed wherever Methodism was established. When Wesley sent leaders to begin work in the American colonies, they took not only their evangelistic zeal but their social consciousness as well. Early American Methodism was a recognized foe of slavery. Methodist preachers were forbidden to own slaves and soon comprised one of the foremost groups to oppose American slavery. Methodist ministers were known for their prophetic preaching and involvement in political and economic issues. This has come to mark Methodism worldwide.

Perhaps nowhere has church or pastoral involvement in the political life of a community or nation been more dramatic than in the ministry of the late Bishop Abel Tendekayi Muzorewa, the Episcopal leader of The United Methodist Church in Zimbabwe. The Rev. Lloyd Nyaraota, in his research of the involvement of Bishop Muzorewa as both religious and political leader, has provided a detailed analysis not only of a political movement but also of the personal journey of Bishop Muzorewa from religious to political leadership. This still-recent history in the development of the country of Zimbabwe needs to be told and shared, as current challenges in the country could so dominate attention that the nation's beginnings could be too quickly forgotten.

It is one thing for a religious leader to confront and challenge political leaders; it is altogether another thing when one becomes a partisan political leader himself. This is what happened in the case of Bishop Abel Tendekayi Muzorewa while serving as a bishop of The United Methodist Church in Zimbabwe. For a religious leader to attempt to navigate both political and

Foreword

religious leadership simultaneously is in some ways to be in uncharted and treacherous waters.

The pages that follow in this well-written and detailed volume is an effort to "look back" on the challenge and complexity of moving from colonialism to independence, to the making of a new independent nation on the continent of Africa. Rev. Lloyd Nyarota critically examines the impact of this gallant attempt of leadership on The United Methodist Church in Zimbabwe, its leader, Bishop Muzorewa, the effort toward nation building, political struggle, and division.

What happens when the prophetic voice expected of and from the church becomes a secular political entity? How does it challenge itself, or how is it distinguished from the political power it seeks to hold accountable on behalf of all the people? How are state and church distinguished? What happens to the prophetic voice of the church and its leadership? These are some of the issues raised and addressed in this timely book. Rev. Nyarota brings theological reflection and critique with the sensitivity of both scholar and churchman.

Equally important to the reader is to get an overview of the challenge and complexity of the movement from protest to governance. How is it possible for a people to move from a disenfranchised status to majority rule in a country where they have so long been denied participation in the affairs of state?

It is to be expected, as Rev. Nyarota attempts to address these questions so filled with partisan and political ramifications, that there will be other views, positions, and recollections of the same events and times. It will and should cause review, assessment, and even debate as these turbulent times are examined.

As a friend and colleague bishop of the late Bishop Abel Tendekayi Muzorewa, for me to read of his personal struggles and challenges—political and religious—was personally a moving and emotional experience. I became a bishop of The United Methodist Church in 1984; by this time Bishop Muzorewa had been a bishop of the church for sixteen years. I came to know him not as political leader but as a colleague, mentor, and friend. I experienced his gentleness, quiet spirit, deep faith, and his sense of calm.

More than twenty-five years ago, during my first visit to Zimbabwe, I traveled with the Bishop across the countryside and saw its breathtaking beauty as he shared stories of its rich history, struggles, and valiant people. It is hard to imagine this man of such slight stature simultaneously carrying

Foreword

upon his shoulders the weight of political struggle, administering the affairs of the church, and offering political leadership to an emerging nation.

Those who know the history of these times, the emergence of the nation of Zimbabwe, and the dynamics in the church and country will read these words from their own context and recollections. It cannot be otherwise. But with the passing of time new insights might be gained as well as a broader perspective on events, the times, and its leadership.

Author Rev. Lloyd Nyarota, in his research resulting in this book, provides the reader the luxury of engaging a turbulent period of the history of a nation, struggles of a people, and the challenges of leadership—political and religious—without taking the risks and making the sacrifices those times required. If the reading of this book and the reliving of these times makes us better citizens of our own native land, more faithful followers of a loving, forgiving, and just God, as well as more committed to a society and world of freedom and justice for all people everywhere, then perhaps the life and witness of Bishop Abel Tendekay Muzorewa will have made its greatest contribution.

Bishop Woodie W. White, Retired
The United Methodist Church
Bishop in Residence, Emory University
Candler School of Theology
July 2011

Definition of Terms

Public arena: National-level political and religious activities.

National struggle: The acts of the indigenous people of Zimbabwe in freeing themselves from the racially oppressive systems of colonialism and white minority rule.

Religious leadership: Nationally-recognized Episcopal level leadership; also nationally-recognized ordained ministers.

Development of religious leadership: Development in response to the demands of a situation at a national level, from the various political dispensations to demands of "the flock," or church membership, personal spiritual interpretation of biblical ethics, and church doctrinal and personal disciplinary requirements of an Episcopal leader.

Open national conflict: The national conflict in Rhodesia during the period under study where the whole indigenous population was involved in one way or the other in a war of liberation against colonial domination.

Religion: The Christian religion unless otherwise specified.

Church: The Christian community as the universal church or as separate institutions or denominations.

State: Refers to government and also national structures.

Episcopal area: The area under one bishop of the United Methodist Church.

1

Introduction

THIS BOOK IS AN analysis of the development of religious leadership in the public arena in response to an open national political conflict. The focus is on the role that Bishop Abel Tendekayi Muzorewa played in Zimbabwe as a major political figure in the nationalist struggle for majority rule while maintaining his Episcopal leadership of The United Methodist Church in Zimbabwe between 1972 and 1980.

The book addresses how religious leaders interpret their mandate in the face of public pressure in an open national political conflict and investigates how far into the political arena a religious leader can go while remaining true to his or her primary call to the ministry. Furthermore, the book addresses the issues rarely mentioned when people narrate how Zimbabwe came into being. Some critical players like Bishop Abel Tendekayi Muzorewa are sidelined and generally demonized in order to distort history. But history speaks for itself.

The traditional relationship of church and state is examined together with related theories of separation. The Rev. Dr. Martin Luther King Jr.'s statement sets the premises for this study: "The church should not be the master or servant or instrument of the state, but it is the conscience of the state."[1]

There are four central observations discussed in this book:

1. Religious leaders have to balance demands from political circles with demands from their church membership. Furthermore, the doctrinal demands from their church traditions further complicate personal choice of action based on spiritual and empirical interpretation. There are, therefore, no easy solutions or set of rules that can guide religious leaders at all times

1. King, *Stride toward Freedom*, 91.

and in all circumstances. One has to think through each situation as it arises. This is especially challenging when one believes that the end does not justify the means. Leaders with high morals would not think any other way.

2. The most effective contribution that can be made by religious leadership to the public arena to resolve national political conflicts is to vigorously influence the moral framework within which decisions are made. This means religious leaders have to make themselves and forcefully make contact with the political leadership (in Gandhi's sense of *satyagraha*—"truth force").

3. Religious leadership is generally seen to be compromised by close association with a party political stance. This is particularly a problem in a political atmosphere where opposing parties view each other as enemies with the intent of exterminating each other. This is true especially in a winner-takes-all situation. Religious leadership that is seen in a competitive light with political powers is deprived of its noble attribute of responding to a higher calling. This is particularly problematic when winning the election is viewed in material terms only.

4. Persons like Bishop Abel Tendekayi Muzorewa, who find themselves being called by their people both to political leadership and the general population to save situations sometimes have no option but to be involved and go the full lap of the race. Unfortunately, once one gets in, one becomes a part of the process. When one realizes what needs to be done, it is difficult to stop before the total mission is accomplished. For this reason, Bishop Abel Tendekayi Muzorewa was so committed to the nation's political freedom that he could not leave the political arena until Zimbabwe was totally free. When he finally resigned, he thought the nation was free, but he had to come back when signs of suppression of the population began to emerge. Until his death, Bishop Abel Tendekayi Muzorewa had one thing he wished for Zimbabwe—total freedom. Unfortunately, he died before true democracy was born. Fortunately, because he was a man of God his prophetic speeches still speak to the nation.

Several challenges presented themselves during the research of this book. The first challenge is the length of time that has elapsed since the period when the events took place. Twenty-five to thirty years have elapsed. Some key informants have grown older and forgotten much of what happened; others have died.

Second, drawing out unbiased information from some of the primary sources was difficult as many of them had shifted their political positions since 1980. Worse still, this research took place at the climax of a campaign for national elections. The Zimbabwean political arena is characteristically heated during an election period when old grudges are often revived. Asking people about events and information about Bishop Abel Tendekayi Muzorewa and just mentioning the UANC might have been misinterpreted as having a hidden agenda. Therefore, not all respondents were free to share the information they knew about the bishop's political and religious leadership.

Third, there is not much literature published on the events that took place during the period under consideration. In addition, even though there is some literature on the general theories of church-state relations, it is the nature of Christian ethics that each historical situation requires a new struggle to seek God's presence and will in that reality. To examine in depth the church's search for ethical norms in situations of open national political conflict would extend far beyond the capacity and scope of this book. Be that as it may, it is an important foundation for understanding the full range of influences on the decision-making process of a church leader when he is presented with challenges of open conflict in the national political arena.

2

Church Leadership and Political Challenges

Religious leadership has critical roles to play during national political conflicts. In this book we seek to share an understanding of the particular role of religious leadership in accomplishing a political process. One often hears declarations such as "This is a Christian country!" or "Don't mix religion and politics!" The general argument is that the church should only be concerned with saving souls and not get into politics. Some theologians would argue that the gospel should transform institutions as well as people's hearts. A host of Christians argue for the principle of the separation of church and state.[1]

In nearly every discussion on religion and politics, arguments like these abound. What do they mean? How do they relate to each other? Jesus said, "Render therefore to Caesar the things that are Caesar's and to God the things that are God's" (Mark 12:17), thereby suggesting that Jesus was approving the existence of government but limiting its dominion. The difficulty comes when trying to decide what actually belongs to Caesar and what should be reserved exclusively for God. How Christians are to understand and apply Jesus's words has been a point of controversy since the days of the early apostles. Should Christians actively participate in government? This and other questions on the role of religious leadership in the political arena will form the background discussion as we look at the role that Bishop Abel T. Muzorewa played in the Liberation of Zimbabwe. In this book we contend that he became a key player and, at one time, the only hope for all blacks. This includes the black nationalists of that time, like Dr. Joshua Nkomo, Mr. Robert Mugabe, Mr. James Chikerema, and Rev. Ndabaningi Sithole, as well

---

1. Eidsmoe, *God and Caesar*, ix.

as southern African leaders like Dr. Kenneth Kaunda of Zambia, Mr. Julius Mwalimu Nyerere of Tanzania, and Mr. Samora Moises Machel of Mozambique, to mention but a few. Except for Rev. Ndabaningi Sithole, Bishop Muzorewa was the only person who played a dual role in church and secular politics simultaneously.

Bishop Abel T. Muzorewa's role as a church leader who was involved in the political dynamics of Zimbabwe from 1972 is rather unique and therefore worthy of special attention. During this period, Bishop Muzorewa was both the Episcopal head of The United Methodist Church and was also involved in the emergence of national political activities of the country as President of the United African National Council (UANC). In 1979 Mr. Ian Smith worked an internal settlement that sidelined the guerilla movements who were fighting to free Zimbabwe. The minority white rule acceded to the sharing of power with three of the nationalist leaders, thereby forming the short-lived Zimbabwe-Rhodesia Government. Bishop Abel T. Muzorewa, as head of the UANC, was one of these three leaders and became the first African Prime Minister of Zimbabwe-Rhodesia.

Church leadership had become unusually prominent in political circles from the 1970s. In fact, going further back in history, on 11 November 1965, when Ian Smith and his Rhodesian Front declared Unilateral Declaration of Independence (UDI) from Britain, the Rhodesians felt they had "struck a blow for the preservation of justice, civilization and Christianity." This immediately raised a challenge for the Christian community and Rhodesia's Christian leaders in particular. Did the "Christian" nature of the Rhodesian Front politics reflect the convictions of the Christian community at large? If not, Christians were faced with a challenge at the political level.

When Smith assumed the office of Prime Minister and declared the colony independent from the British, African nationalists also stepped up their demands for the independents from white rule, resulting in one of the most bitter conflicts in Africa. This war was fought over moral principles. How could the religious leadership have refrained from stepping in when the majority of Zimbabweans were denied all human rights?

Bishop Muzorewa was brought into the political arena by the events of the time. The All Africa Conference of Churches held a series of major consultations to discuss the churches' stance on national liberation struggles in various African nations. In fact, other religious leaders of Zimbabwe were also deeply involved in the nationalist struggle. For instance, two other outstanding religious leaders who gained fame for their contribution to the political struggle were Rev. Canaan Banana of the Methodist Church in Zimbabwe, who later became the ceremonial President of Zimbabwe in 1980, and Rev. Ndabaningi Sithole, who was the founder of the Zimbabwe African National Unity (ZANU), which eventually won the national election in 1980 and has continued as the ruling party to date.

In the rest of this book, our discussion revolves around Bishop Muzorewa's role in the national struggle for Zimbabwe's liberation as well as his role as a religious leader in the national political conflicts. Three major sources that influenced the way Bishop Muzorewa interpreted his public leadership role will be examined:

- the influence of his church's constitution and doctrine, and the Bishop's own perceptions of his moral and ethical vocation for public engagement in resolving the national conflict;
- the expectations, perceptions and demands of the political activists of his time;
- the perceptions and demands of his church members, who constituted his primary reference group.

Also, from Bishop Muzorewa's actions and involvement in the political conflict, some general observations about the possibilities and limitations of other religious leaders in national political conflicts will be pointed out. By making this historical record and acknowledging what this particular man of God sacrificed and fought for, it is hoped that this book will inspire other religious leaders. Furthermore, it is hoped that certain lessons can emerge from this discourse. For instance,

- how religious leaders can help to resolve conflict;
- the ethics that should govern religious leaders in the public arena in relation to national political conflicts;
- making ethical decisions concerning involvement in the political realm while remaining faithful to one's pastoral call and duties.

The life of Bishop Muzorewa and his commitment to the freedom of all people of Zimbabwe is a model for Christians when faced with situations that demand choices in national political conflicts and the freedom of the people.

As noted earlier, if the church is not the master or the servant of the state but the conscience of the state—the guide and critic of the state and never its instrument—then the question is, If a church leader simultaneously takes up the post of head of state, how does Dr. Martin Luther King Jr.'s dictum unfold? The life of Bishop Muzorewa provided a case where Dr. King's theory had to be tested. What forces of influence come to bear in shaping such leadership, which enable it to sustain that vital role which Dr. King calls "the conscience of the state"?

Bishop Muzorewa had to deal with questions such as:

- How do religious leaders interpret their mandate in the face of public pressure in an open national conflict?
- What contribution can religious leadership make in the public arena that would help to resolve an open national political conflict?
- How far into the political arena can religious leaders go and still be helpful in resolving a national conflict while remaining true to their primary calling?
- How can a Prophet prophesy to himself (as head of state and head of the church)?
- When is the opportune moment to let go?

Put differently, all these questions could be summarized in a phrase: How spiritual and how political can one become without either neglecting or betraying the other, or even possibly both? Bishop Muzorewa gives us a case scenario.

3

The Political Call

It is important to first establish how Bishop Muzorewa came into the political arena. What made him make the decision that he was going to be involved in the national political crisis? Could he have sat back and watched, only minding his church business?

Some historians have pointed out that the Bishop came in to unify all the nationalist leaders in the struggle for freedom and independence in Zimbabwe as they were pulling in different directions and for personal gain. Ariston Chambati notes that the African National Council (ANC) during the period 1971–79 occupies an important place in the history of the liberation movements regardless of its negative and dysfunctional aspects at a later stage in its development.[1] It was through the ANC that Bishop Muzorewa formally entered national politics. In 1971 the British government and the Rhodesian regime under Ian Smith's Rhodesian Front ruling party held constitutional talks in Harare (then Salisbury) known as the Smith-Home talks. African people were excluded from the talks even though it was primarily their future at stake. The proposals that emerged from these talks contained a central principle: National Independence to Rhodesia by Majority Acceptance (NIBMA), which required a test of acceptability by all the people. When Africans became aware of this principle, they agreed. Their strategy was to mobilize themselves to reject the proposals on the basis that they had not been part of the process.[2] And, more important, it was unacceptable for the sovereignty of the new nation-state to be founded on the basis and terms of minority rule.

1. Chambati, "National Unity-ANC," 147.
2. Ibid.

The Political Call

The British government, in collaboration with the white Rhodesian regime, decided to appoint a British controlled commission to test the acceptability of the constitutional proposals. The commission was appointed under the chairmanship of Lord Pearce, hence the label "the Pearce Commission." This is how Bishop Muzorewa found himself involved in political leadership:

> The African people believed that only through a political organization would they succeed in mobilizing themselves for a "No" vote at the referendum. Joshua Nkomo, the veteran nationalist who was in detention during this time, wrote, "In preparation for the Pearce Commission, I communicated with Garfield Todd[3] to insure that his opposition would be expressed in terms similar to ours. I also got in touch with Josiah Chinamano,[4] who had by now been released, in order to set up a front organization to coordinate African opposition. On his suggestion we approached a well-known churchman, Methodist Bishop Abel Muzorewa. He seemed an ideal candidate for the treasurer of the new body, which we decided to call the African National Council. If a Bishop couldn't raise money, who can? It was soon suggested that, since the Bishop was a political novice, while Josiah was closely identified with me, the Council's appeal could be broadened if the Bishop became Chairman while Josiah acted as Treasurer. I readily agreed, and this was the start of poor Abel Muzorewa's illusion that he had become a political leader.[5]

This excerpt from Nkomo's autobiography suggests that it was at Nkomo's suggestion that the ANC was created as a front organization to oppose the Smith-Home proposals, and Bishop Muzorewa was in the plan only to be used as a churchman to raise money for the work of the politicians. However, Chinamano had a different thought: it was his idea to have Bishop Muzorewa as chairman since he was a political novice not targeted by Smith's government. Nkomo never saw Bishop Muzorewa as a political leader. The Bishop was only being invited into the ANC as a defense wall against the Smith regime and to give credibility to the new organization. They wanted him for that reason, nothing more or less, according to Nkomo.

---

3. He was a former Church of Christ missionary who had become a politician and was elected to be prime minister of Rhodesia. But because of his liberal policy he was ousted by the Rhodesia Front from power and was now in support of the African nationalists' cause for majority rule.

4. One of the founding members of the nationalist movement, and Vice President of Nkomo's ZAPU.

5. Nkomo, *Nkomo*, 143–44.

Religious Leadership in National Political Conflicts

But what terms were spelled out to Bishop Muzorewa when he was invited to lead the ANC? This approach to politics has continued in Zimbabwe where individuals position themselves as the sole leaders of national issues and the nation, and all other people are just viewed as means to an end. Nkomo had no idea that Bishop Muzorewa was an intelligent person capable of a mind of his own. Not only did Nkomo underestimate the man of God, but the Smith regime also made the same mistake.

The ANC was formed on December 16, 1971, as a vehicle through which African political thought could be expressed on that decisive referendum, which was to take place in early 1972. Thus all African political organizations representing various shades of opinion agreed to come together under the umbrella of the ANC for the purpose of rejecting the 1971 Anglo-Rhodesian constitutional proposals. The unity goal underlying the formation of this new organization was embodied in the ANC constitution, whose objective was to mobilize the African people to appreciate that the power of unity, and the need to explain, advise on, and expose the dangerous implications of the 1971 Anglo-Rhodesian constitutional proposals.[6]

Most political leaders at that time were in detention, but even if they had been free, would they have been able to unite the people of Zimbabwe at this crucial hour of their struggle for democracy? This became a dicey issue and contributed to the choice of Bishop Muzorewa as leader of the new organization. It was the general feeling among the Africans that if the new organization was led by one of the people previously associated with the banned political parties, the Rhodesian regime would consider the ANC to be a revival of these banned parties and would immediately force it out of existence. Also, the architects of the organization shared the view that the leader should be a person who was not involved in the conflict between the banned political parties, lest the majority of the African people decline to join the new organization. In choosing a church leader and one who was a well-known orator, it was believed that the population would rally behind him regardless of their past political affiliations—a one-time noble decision! The political leaders in detention were divided on their own as the parties had split. There were fights for leadership between Joshua Nkomo and those who had formed ZANU. Moreover, ZANU was in the process of fighting for leadership within itself. Due to these political divisions the people of Zimbabwe were divided among themselves, and there was a serious conflict amongst the nationalists.

---

6. Chambati, "National Unity," 147.

The Political Call

Some regarded Bishop Muzorewa as leader acting in place of the detained African nationalist leaders.[7] The Bishop himself is said to have testified that his choice to accept leadership of a political umbrella group in the build-up to the referendum was for the sake of the achievement of unity. In the *Rhodesia Herald* of February 27, 1972, he is reported to have said, "I was astonished that many people of different political views should come and ask me to be their leader. I considered their request for two weeks before deciding to go along with them."[8] These were two weeks of specially focused prayer and consulting the church structures. Bishop Muzorewa was a person who always consulted before taking action. The people encouraged him to help and save his nation at this critical time. Ian Smith had to be stopped. Zimbabwe had to be saved, and the Bishop was the identified leader to carry this national task. One may have to guess how many times the Bishop must have sung his favorite hymn.

Chambati noted that during his early leadership days, Bishop Muzorewa told people that he was not the real leader of the Africans but was merely acting on behalf of the African nationalist leaders who were in detention. This position would have been correct if the leaders had become united toward one purpose. The Bishop was prepared to hand over leadership to an "Aaron" or a "Joshua" if there was one.

Announcing the formation of the ANC at a press conference in December 1971 in Highfield, the Bishop attacked and denounced the Smith-Home constitutional proposals and said that African people condemned the manner in which the British Government had conducted the 1971 Anglo-Rhodesian discussions. The participants had totally ignored the African people. Thus, the ANC was the embodiment of a united front that embraced various political parties, notably the Zimbabwe African National Unity (ZANU) and the Zimbabwe African People's Union (ZAPU), and which also represented the liberation movements associated with these two parties, ZANLA and ZIPRA.[9]

At this point nothing but unity could save the situation in Rhodesia. ZANU and ZAPU could not do it, hence a new Front with focused leadership toward the liberation of the people. This is how Bishop Muzorewa became the center player.

C. Nyangoni and G. Nyandoro assess that the investigation of African attitudes to the Smith-Home settlement proposals by the Pearce

---

7. Ibid., 148.
8. *The Rhodesia Herald*, February 27, 1972.
9. Chambati, "National Unity," 148.

Religious Leadership in National Political Conflicts

Commission was the first opportunity since 1890 that Africans had ever had regarding crucial national matters.[10] Needless to say, the people of Zimbabwe at this point needed genuine leadership focusing on them as a people, not self-serving politicians. Leaders who were in prison at this time were at the mercy of the vindictive government rather than at their people's service. A new situation was created where the shared concerns of different African organizations converged. The unanimous rejection of Smith's attempt to get his illegal Unilateral Declaration of Independence (UDI) internationally recognized and entrenched conditionally led to the birth of a new united political force from within Rhodesia, the ANC, led by Bishop Muzorewa, albeit a novice nationalist.

In its interim committee of December 1971, there were other articulate churchmen such as Canaan Banana and H. H. Kachidza, both ordained preacher-politicians who recently had been released from detention together with activists like Ruth and Josiah Chinamano, Edison Sithole, and Edison Zvobgo.[11] Commenting on the formation of the ANC, Ian Smith observed:

> The black extremists had reorganized themselves under the banner of the newly formed ANC with the same leaders in positions of authority, but they had introduced an astute new ruse to cover up the old faces, which were still tainted by association with the intimidation and petrol bombing. They brought in Abel Muzorewa, the first black man ever to have been made a Bishop in Rhodesia, and made him the leader of the new party, thus giving themselves a much more acceptable face of respectability.[12]

This indicates that even according to Ian Smith, the Bishop gave the African majority the respect they deserved and the power that helped them to fight against the proposals. Ian Smith was hoping to capitalize on the divisions of the ZANU-ZAPU leadership to have it his way. Nationalists who had been at each other's throats, rather than focusing on the main thing, were now untied and more powerful, posing a real threat to Ian Smith. The coming of a sober and selfless figure (Bishop Abel Tendekayi Muzorewa) surprised the British. The British were also caught unaware by this political maneuver by Africa as a whole. It does not take rocket science to realize how true the old adage is: united we stand, divided we fall.

10. Nyangoni andNyandoro, *Zimbabwe Independent Movements*, 1.
11. Hellencreutz, *Religion and Politics*, 417.
12. Smith, *Bitter Harvest*, 154.

The Political Call

At this point, the churches encouraged their religious leaders to step into the national political arena boldly. The Christian Council of Rhodesia (CCR) at its meeting on September 8, 1971, affirmed that settlement proposals had to satisfy basic moral criteria of justice and human rights. These would have to be written in the constitution and be defendable in the courts of law. For instance, there must be no first and second class citizenship. All people must have full and equal rights.[13] Following the CCR executive meeting on December 30, 1971, the CCR held a meeting at the University of Rhodesia chaired by the ex-president of CCR, the Rev A. M. Ndhlela. Among the attendees were both the president and vice president of the newly constituted ANC, Bishop Abel T. Muzorewa and the Rev C. Banana, as well as the Rev H. H. Kachidza, who would succeed Josiah Chinamano as the ANC treasurer. Bishop Donald Lamont, an outspoken critic of the Smith regime who was eventually placed under house arrest, was among the Roman Catholic observers. After considerable discussion, the CCR declared: "In light of the serious defects in the proposals for a settlement, it is our considerable judgment that they should be rejected."[14] Later the Bishop's own denomination, The United Methodist Church Annual Conference, supported the ANC's position as the official organization representing African aspirations.[15]

The central issue as far as Bishop Abel Muzorewa was concerned was equality of all people irrespective of race or political opinion. Unfortunately, to this day, the same battle is still on today; Zimbabweans are persecuted for their political opinions. This is because most African leaders equate political opposition with enmity. Leadership that is insecure tends to spend more energy witch-hunting than focusing on national leadership. But Bishop Muzorewa was different.

After his presentation of evidence to the Pearce Commission in mid-1972, the Bishop traveled to the United Kingdom and the United States of America, ostensibly to sell the ANC's point of view. He informed the British and the Americans that the African people rejected the Anglo-Rhodesian constitutional proposals and warned that any attempt to impose these proposals on them would lead to a bloodbath in Rhodesia. While in London, the Bishop held a number of meetings with politicians, journalists, and Rhodesian Africans, aimed at giving a true picture of the situation in Rhodesia.[16]

13. Christian Council of Rhodesia, Council Meeting minutes of September 8, 1971.

14. Christian Council of Rhodesia, Council Meeting minutes of December 30, 1971.

15. Official Journal of the Rhodesia Annual Conference of The United Methodist Church (1973), 86–87.

16. Chambati, "National Unity," 150.

Religious Leadership in National Political Conflicts

The Bishop was a consultative nationalist leader. He tried to consult all the people, both those in the country and those in Diaspora, on the developments that were taking place at home. He also consulted with the British, who were major stakeholders at the time, as well as with the Americans. Could it be that it was this style of leadership that earned him the support of all the nationalists of various parties?

It is believed that the day the Pearce Commission left Rhodesia after their work was completed is when the ANC became a permanent organization. Bishop Muzorewa was asked to continue as its leader in the capacity of president. Again the religious leader was being asked to continue his political role with the blessing of the nationalists. This was due to the type of leadership the people of Zimbabwe had tasted during the Pearce Commission. The African-Rhodesians had learned that they could be united, that they could work together instead of fighting themselves. Zimbabweans had a taste of what it is to be led toward a goal of liberation and self-determination. They were led to this awareness by one simple clergyman's leadership style.

In search of a negotiated settlement, the Bishop held several meetings with Ian Smith in 1973. But Ian Smith was not sincere in his negotiations, and the ANC followers became suspicious and anxious that the Bishop was being used by the regime to fulfill Smith's agenda. However, at a special meeting of the ANC held in September 1973, according to Chambati, the Bishop was also given a mandate to continue negotiating with the Smith regime to achieve majority rule in Zimbabwe. At the end of 1973, in his Christmas message the Bishop stated that the ANC remained united and faithful to its goal of achieving a peaceful and just society. He also stated that the most important lesson that the ANC had learned from his talks with Ian Smith was that it was possible for all people in Rhodesia to come together and talk about their differences with a view to building a just society.[17]

A further mandate was given to him at the ANC inaugural conference in March 1974. Many observers described this congress as the largest African nationalist gathering in Zimbabwe for more than ten years. People came to the congress to plan for their movement toward independence as a united force under the leadership of committed nationalists. The ANC had become a symbol of the people's aspirations. Both ZANU and ZAPU former supporters had realized that Bishop Muzorewa was a leader focused on national interests. They were ready to be led. People questioned policies without fear. The congress made decisions without being coerced. Bishop Muzorewa went to the Congress ready to listen to the peoples' wishes as

17. Ibid., 152.

a nation. In that spirit, the congress asked the Bishop to go ahead leading them and negotiating with the regime so that the people could achieve a just society—freedom and justice for all. The meeting provided a forum for ANC leaders and their followers to raise questions about the policies of the organization. Once more, the congress reaffirmed the Bishop's leadership and gave the ANC a mandate to continue negotiations with the Smith regime.[18] The people had faith in the Bishop that he would look after everyone's interest as a good leader should, not just personal interests, as had been the case with other leaders. In a space of six months, therefore, the Bishop was twice given the ANC's mandate to lead, and Rev. Canaan Banana was elected his vice president. Moreover, he was mandated to use a nonviolent approach to find a solution to resolve the national conflict through negotiated settlement. It is after receiving this mandate that some nationalists began to say that he seemed to get carried away and began to make decisions without consulting the people. As a result, the Bishop lost the support of some of his constituents.

In actual fact, it was at this time when self-centered nationalists realized that the people were beginning to realize the real objectives of nationalism and that they were losing power and followers. Hence, they began to confuse people again with the ZANU-ZAPU rhetoric and began the politics of blackmailing and condemning each other. Now the main target was the Bishop who alone was focused on national interests. Those in prison felt they were losing ground. In actual fact, they were fighting even in prison. There were coups going on within ZANU even though they were in prison. The focus was self-interest and leadership. The Rev. Ndabaningi Sithole was couped while in prison. Many of those who argued that the Bishop was getting carried away because he was no longer consulting them were in prison. The ZANU-ZAPU leadership wanted the Bishop to act as their puppet and not as a real leader of the people. But the majority of Zimbabweans had enough confidence in the Bishop that he would lead them toward majority rule. For those in prison, the Bishop was advancing beyond his mandate; they expected the people to get their final decisions endorsed by them. This tension between the Bishop and several nationalists has not waned since then. That is what has created the legacy we have today no matter what Zimbabweans decide to do. Robert Mugabe in his individual capacity must have the final voice; that is the reason why today ZANU (PF) cannot make a decision no matter what people want; word comes from Robert G. Mugabe. He is ZANU (PF) and has the final say. Suffice it to say, such was not Bishop

18. Ibid.

Religious Leadership in National Political Conflicts

Muzorewa's leadership style. Could it be that this difference in leadership is influenced by a theological rather than nationalist orientation? Put differently, is Bishop Muzorewa's leadership style a reflection of his other career as an Episcopal leader? Are church and politics exclusive of each other? Bishop Muzorewa seems to have been the embodiment of the two disciplines. This leads us to the next chapter on church and state.

4

Church and State

THE PROBLEM OF CHURCH and state goes back to the ages of the Roman empire, when Christianity began to be a power to be reckoned with. It is a power or authority issue. At the root is the tension between two authorities: one representing claims made in the name of political regimes, the other representing claims in the name of the Almighty. These patterns of dual authority structures and the variety of relationships between them have been explored more fully in western Christian history than elsewhere.[1] In this book, the phenomenon is dealt with in the context of Zimbabwean liberation struggle, thereby making it rather dramatic and radical.

In the Roman empire Christianity developed slowly as a distinctive movement regarded with suspicion by the authorities. It was not long before it was involved in direct institutional conflict with the imperial authority (Rev. 13) over issues of authority. In the year 313 AD, with the Edict of Milan, Christianity eventually gained full rights as a religion through the emperor. During the reign of Constantine the Great, a decade later, the church made a major shift from being seen as the enemy of the empire to gaining privileged status.

Accordingly, in its first three centuries, the Christian movement was preoccupied with retaining religious identity and securing social integrity. Thereafter, the church, which had suffered at the hands of government for decades, became united with it. A degree of coexistence took form when Constantine became a Christian. One might wonder whether at that point the emperor had become the embodiment of church and state, if that were

---

1. Wilson, "Church and State," *Encarta* 2002.

Religious Leadership in National Political Conflicts

possible. If we fast forward through the centuries to the Reformation, we see another instructive scenario regarding church and state.[2]

Let us take a brief look at the Reformation in Europe. In general, Protestant religious groups, particularly the Lutherans and Calvinists, aligned themselves with local and national political authorities in northern Europe during the Reformation period, thus encouraging the emergence of modern national communities. Church-state issues were transferred to the level of national communities. However, the temporary solution to the religious conflict in Europe was the Peace of Augsburg (1555), which stipulated that each political entity should establish either Lutheranism or Roman Catholicism as a "religious monopoly."[3]

Again, we raise the rhetorical question: Was this an embodiment of the two authorities? Missionaries played a role in the colonial process. The example of the Ruddy concession comes to mind.

Another look at the modern period shows a general pattern emerging in more recent European societies in which churches are free to develop their own programs, even where a political group has been legally established. Wilson makes the observation,

> Where separate authority structures exist, many relationships are possible. At one extreme is the subordination of political to religion, as in a (hierocracy), or rule of priests as the guardians of divine mysteries. The other extreme entails subordination of the religious institutions to the political regime, as in Caesaropapism. Between these extremes are various relationships ranging from an Erastian, or state-dominated, church to a theocratic political order, in which rulers are closely monitored by guardians of the dominant religious tradition.[4]

The phrase "church and state" represents a framework for understanding how religion and government are related when these different institutions make formal claims not only within the same society but with same constituents. The substance of this interaction exists in most societies. Where the respective claims of religion and politics have not been clearly focused in separate institutions, religious and political struggles have been no less real.

The Latin American churches' struggle to liberate themselves from partnership with oppressive oligarchies produced significant theological

2. Ibid.
3. Ibid.
4. Ibid.

body of thought termed "liberation theology." Gustavo Gutiérrez, in his classic book *A Theology of Liberation,* sees the deep causes of the 1970s social reality and realizes that these had to be attacked if there was to be radical change and real, meaningful peace and justice. This, says Gutierrez, necessarily implies confrontation in which various forms of violence are present between groups with different interests. This in turn makes demands that may seem difficult or disturbing to those who wish to achieve or maintain a low-cost conciliation. Such conciliation can only be a justifying ideology for a profound disorder, a device for the few to keep living off the poverty of the many. To be aware that in politics conflict is inevitable means "struggling with clarity and courage, deceiving neither oneself nor others for the establishment of peace and justice among all people."[5] In the past, theology had not sufficiently taken into account its role in the political dimension of society; it had been complacent about political, social, and economic structures and concerned itself only with spiritual life and moral values. But Latin American liberation theology has since made the church realize its holistic, liberating mission in society. Liberation theology prepared the ground for the church's involvement in the political arena without a sense of intrusion. The African church drew much of its inspiration from Latin American liberation theology although their circumstances were slightly different.

Individual Christians and Christian communities are not exempt from the temptation to play it safe and expect others to do the hard and dangerous work. The example of Jesus Christ makes it clear that a mediator cannot remain neutral and that the work of confrontation for the sake of reconciliation is bound to be supremely costly. Tracy Honor, in one of her books, quotes the exhortation of an Irish parish priest to his flock to "tread the straight and narrow path between right and wrong." Once the religious leader contemplates confrontational situations, decisions between right and wrong will have to be made, though this is often easier said than done.[6]

Bishop Muzorewa tried to walk this "straight and narrow path between right and wrong." He could not remain neutral. He had to take a side, and in 1972 he took the side of the oppressed and became president of the ANC in its struggle for freedom. There simply was no one else suitable to take up that task. Even the nationalists voted for him to lead the nation! The nation could have been granted independence by the British under the Smith regime, and sanctions would immediately have been lifted to please the very small white minority at the expense of the African majority. Rhodesia would

---

5. Gutiérrez, *Theology of Liberation*, 48.
6. Honor, *Straight and Narrow Path*.

have become recognized as an independent state in the world even though the majority was not free. It would have been a nation established on the unacceptable principles of racism and injustice. Rhodesia would have become a recognized apartheid system that would have become difficult to dismantle. But by the grace of God, the Bishop saved the situation by taking up political leadership in addition to church leadership. Being the first African Bishop of any denomination in Zimbabwe, he felt the pressure to meet the challenge at this *kairos* moment in the history of the nation. Since he was not a veteran politician or nationalist, he was bound to make some mistakes. (This is not to imply that veteran politicians do not make any mistakes.)

To speak meaningfully about reconciliation, one cannot ignore its shadow side. The shadow side is conflict—conflict of presuppositions, interests, and political aspirations. None of these may be ignored if there is to be a prospect of real peace and true reconciliation. Perhaps the greatest failure of the church is that it has almost always tried to make peace, and to pretend that peace exists, when the underlying current is not resolved. In the political, social, and economic spheres, these are generally issues of social justice.[7] Thus in the Old Testament, the prophet Jeremiah reproached the religious leaders of his own day: "From prophet to priest every one deals falsely. They have healed the wounds of my people lightly, saying, 'Peace, peace,' when there is no peace" (Jer. 6:13–14). These words are echoed in one of Jesus's les-than-soothing sayings: "Do you think that I have come to give peace on earth? No, I tell you, but rather division" (Luke 12:51)—or, as Matthew has recorded it, "a sword" (Matt. 10:34). Reconciliation is costly, yet it is worth it.

The failure of the church to be more than just a voice appealing for peace comes from looking for what Gutiérrez called "low-cost conciliation."

> There is no way of avoiding the sword of confrontation and conflict if there is to be a true meeting of opponents. The dialogue may be fierce, even unavoidably violent, but only on that condition is there any possibility of reaching a degree of mutual respect and understanding, and ultimately, of genuine reconciliation. That is not to make light of the costs that a resort to violence brings with it, the sufferings of the innocent, the hardening of hearts of those who become habituated to it, above all the way in which violence leads to further violence in its turn.[8]

---

7. De Waal, *Politics of Reconciliation*, 68.
8. Gutiérrez, *Theology of Liberation*, 50.

A violent confrontation is always fruitless, but violence endured while working for true reconciliation usually results in a meaningful and lasting peace with dignity and both respect for each other and self-respect.

The way of nonviolence is not a means of avoiding conflict; indeed it invites it, as its greatest protagonists, Gandhi and Martin Luther King Jr., knew only too well. Nonviolence may be a higher way than the resort to violence, but neither avoids the necessity of confrontation.

Theologians such as Walter Rauschenbusch (1975) have severely criticized the view, dominant in the church for over fifteen hundred years, that the world is essentially evil and that withdrawal from it is the only way to practice the authentic Christian life. Rauschenbusch argued that such a stance was irresponsible for the modern Christian. For him there were only two alternatives: the church must both condemn the world and seek to change it, or tolerate the world and conform to it.[9] He advocated the former course, insisting that the Christians are charged to transform the world rather than conform to it.[10]

Martin Luther King Jr., whose theological reflection on the church's responsibility in the public domain also had tremendous influence on African ecclesiastical thinking in the 1960s and 1970s, thought Rauschenbusch had done a great service for the church by insisting that the gospel deals with the whole person, not only the soul. It must address the social, political, and economic conditions in which one lives.[11] Dr. King was convinced of the tenacity of evil in the social structures of society and the requirements of power to overcome the forces of evil. This insight inspired Dr. King to justify the use of power by churchmen through nonviolent direct action.[12] Dr. King is one of very few church men who literally transformed society through the gospel. More than that, he also transformed the American political atmosphere through nonviolent direct action. Was this a case of church and state converging in the ministry of Dr. King?

Scholars such as Brian Johansson, who wrote from the South African experience of the 1970s, noted, "The ideal state, from the perspective of the church, would be the state that is governed in obedience to God, and it is remarkable how, in the providence of God, human governments do have a considerable knowledge of what is right."[13]

9. Rauschenbusch, *Christianity and the Social Crisis*, 342.
10. Ibid., 352.
11. King, *Stride toward Freedom*, 91.
12. Smith, *Bitter Harvest*, 136.
13. Johansson, *Church and State*, 4–5.

Religious Leadership in National Political Conflicts

Throughout history, when a person is empowered by God, there is evidence of wisdom and power that transforms society. "This knowledge can be sharpened and clarified through heeding the proclamation of the church. This would in no sense place the church over the state, but would emphasize the fact that both the church and the state are under the authority of God."[14]

One of the great theologians of Germany, Dietrich Bonhoeffer, has had tremendous influence on modern thinking regarding church-state relations due to his martyrdom, which resulted from his direct political action to stop Nazi domination, an approach deeply grounded in his spiritual theology. He writes, "Government and Church are connected in such various ways that their relationship cannot be regulated in accordance with any single general principle. Neither the separation of state and Church, nor the form of the State Church, can, in itself, constitute a solution to the problem. Nothing is more dangerous than to draw theoretical conclusions by generalizing from single particular experiences."[15] He goes on to explain, "No constitutional form can as such exactly represent the actual relative closeness and remoteness of government and Church. Government and Church are bound by the same Lord and are bound together."[16]

This would be the case whether the state acknowledges God as sovereign or not. Bonhoeffer adds,

> In their task government and Church are separate, but government and Church have the same field of action, man. No single one of these relationships must be isolated so as to provide the basis for a particular constitutional form (for example in the sequence state Church, free Church, National Church); the true aim is to provide room within every given form for the relationship which is, in fact, instituted by God and to entrust the further development to the Lord of both government and Church."[17]

This statement gives witness to the complexity of the church-state relation with regard to authority and accountability.

We concur with Dr. King's view that "the church should not be the master, the servant or instrument of the state, but it is the conscience of the state." In 1963 at Kampala, the All Africa Conference of Churches made a significant statement about African nationalism, which reflected some of

---

14. Ibid.
15. Bonhoeffer, *Ethics*, 315.
16. Ibid.
17. Ibid.

this global theological thinking about church and state. The Conference defined nationalism as "the common desire of a people to work together for their emancipation from any form of bondage, whether colonial, economic, social or racial."[18] Four forms of nationalism were distinguished: nationalism working toward freedom and independence; nationalism working toward the creation of national cohesion (particularly important for newly independent nations); nationalism of older nations which, even when repudiated, manifested itself through the attempt to conserve the traditional way of life; and nationalism that evolves into an ideology of totalitarian character, for example, national socialism. Two factors were brought up in the attempt to understand nationalism from an African Christian viewpoint. (1) History is both a past to be preserved and a task to be undertaken. Theologically it was emphasized that history was always the object of God's rule where human obedience is expected. (2) Authority is the goal of emancipation for the responsibility of nationhood. The authority envisaged is exercised by God over nations and entrusted to nations. The assembly perceived that God at times could use historical movements such as nationalism as an instrument of divine rule.

In the interest of reason and balance, it is necessary to define the limits within which nationalism might be a form of Christian obedience and beyond which it could become demonic. Thus, the conference composed the following statement:

> Nationalism must aim at the establishment of freedom and justice and respect of human dignity, instead of being concerned for power for its sake. It must work for the unity and cohesion of the nation, instead of serving the power of one group at the expense of others. However, this does not mean the exclusion of a strong authority, but it does mean that strong authority must not work for the exclusive benefit of one group of the community. At its best, nationalism should be open to and concerned about the establishment of international solidarity instead of expressing the will to dominate other nations even in the name of democracy."[19]

Kampala based the statement above upon the experiences of African churches not only with nationalism but also with the Christian faith. In other words, the church in Africa did not seek to isolate itself from the social, political, economic, and cultural issues that its member nations were facing, for this was where God might need them more—in the ministry of

18. All Africa Conference of Churches, *Drumbeats from Kampala*, 60.
19. Ibid., 60–61.

reconciliation. This understanding of nationalism was to serve as a guiding principle not only for the religious leaders of Zimbabwe who were to be involved in nationalism, but all African leaders in both nationalist and ecclesiastical circles. One always has to bear in mind that in many respects national politics or economy can affect the people's health and morale; similarly, the people's spirituality does affect and influence their economic and political productivity. The African view of life is generally holistic.

5

Toward a Political Career

IN HIS AUTOBIOGRAPHY, BISHOP Muzorewa writes that he started his Christian ministry in the church as an evangelist before he went for more formal theological training at Old Mutare Mission. He served as pastor at the Muziti United Methodist Church, his home area. This area is one of the least productive areas in Rhodesia's Tribal Trust Lands to which black Rhodesians were confined. In 1958 he was sent to the United States for higher education. Upon his return he worked with the Christian Council of Rhodesia as Director of the Student Christian Movement (SCM) serving all denominations. During that period he discussed the nation's political challenges with students in high schools and colleges across the country. The young Reverend Muzorewa developed his skill as a talented orator, and his popularity grew throughout the country. This would contribute to his election to the episcopacy in The United Methodist Church in 1968, making him the first African Bishop ever to be elected in Zimbabwe.[1] Who knew that the very man would become the first African head of state for Zimbabwe?

His denomination had always sympathized with the cause and efforts of African nationalism if it meant freedom from white rule, a nationalism that aimed at establishing freedom, justice, and respect for human dignity for all citizens. In keeping with the spirit of the Christian faith, nationalism was viewed as a way that nationalism became a blessing and not a curse to the nation.[2] Interestingly enough, even Ian Smith implied that being

---

1. Muzorewa, *Rise Up and Walk*, 54–58.
2. Kurewa, *Church in Mission*, 116.

Christian was consistent with being a good citizen. But one suspects that what Smith meant by "a good citizen" was probably different from what the general African populace meant.

The Social Principles of The United Methodist Church clearly state,

> The strength of a political system depends upon the full and willing participation of its citizens. We believe that the state should not attempt to control the Church, nor should the church seek to dominate the state. Separation of Church and state means no organic union of the two, but it does permit interaction. The church should continually exert a strong ethical influence upon the state, supporting policies and programs deemed to be just and opposing policies and programs that are unjust.[3]

Furthermore, United Methodists "support the separation of Church and state." The rightful and vital separation of Church and state, which has served the cause of religious liberty, should not be misconstrued as the abolition of all religious expression from public life.[4]

Bishop Muzorewa's Episcopal predecessor, Bishop Ralph E. Dodge, had launched a program to deliberately cultivate an educated leadership that was aimed at national empowerment. He once noted, "If The United Methodist Church would be true to its heritage and calling, it must minister to the felt needs of people everywhere, and in so doing bring them under the redemptive influence of the gospel." Bishop Dodge believed that "there is power in the gospel to redeem individuals and to restructure society."[5] In fact, he openly challenged the unjust laws of the Rhodesian regime and spoke against discrimination. This resulted in his expulsion from Rhodesia by the Smith regime in 1964. But that was too late because Dodge had sent many Africans to study in the United States. Bishop Muzorewa was one of those who benefited from Bishop Dodge's educational program for African leadership. That Bishop Muzorewa became Bishop Dodge's successor was a rather providential coincidence!

It is clear from this background that The United Methodist Church was not ashamed to be involved in the nationalist effort to overcome the injustice of white minority rule in Rhodesia. This kind of mindset enabled several of its clergy and lay leaders to be involved in the struggle for political freedom and independence for their own people. Since anybody was free

---

3. The United Methodist Church Social Principles, 1997–2000, 27–28.
4. Ibid., 2005–2008, 31.
5. Dodge, *Revolutionary Bishop*, 185–86.

to affiliate with the political party of one's choice, The United Methodist Church never officially aligned itself with one political view or party as a body; instead its official stand was to support nationalism in a broad sense, as long as that nationalism worked for self-respect, dignity, and integrity for every person, a nationalism that was not simply an exchange of masters, but one that worked toward genuine and total freedom and independence for the people of Zimbabweans as a whole.[6] Obviously, with Muzorewa as their bishop, most Methodists had a better grasp of the issues at stake, though no one was ever coerced to support Muzorewa's party.

This was the springboard from which people identified Bishop Muzorewa of The United Methodist as a political leader in the 1970s. The Social Principles of The United Methodist Church clearly state, "The strength of a political system depends upon the full and willing participation of its citizens. The state is not expected to control the Church, nor should the church dominate the state." So, for Bishop Muzorewa, the two entities were separate but equally important in people's lives. Separation of Church and state means no organic union of the two.[7] The Social Principles also state, "The United Methodist Church has for many years supported the separation of Church and state."[8] These are the theories adopted by the Bishop. This book discusses how the religious leadership in Zimbabwe developed to respond to the national conflict, which faced racial, social, and economic as well as political problems.

After several years of political leadership, Bishop Muzorewa retired in the realm of politics but continued his pastoral duties whenever he was called upon to serve. But even after his retirement in political circles, he continued to be an advocate of peace and justice. He believed that all Zimbabweans are God's children. Although Bishop did not lead his nation to complete liberation, history can never deny him credit for the role he played as a selfless leader; one who would rather be fair than make enemies; one who would rather make peace than cause bloodshed.

---

6. Kurewa, *Church in Mission*, 119–20.
7. The United Methodist Church Social Principles, 1997–2000, 27–28.
8. Ibid., 2005–2008, 31.

6

The Formation of the United African National Council (1975)

ACTIVITIES RELATED TO THE development of events from December 1974, with the birth of the United African National Council (UANC), which was later popularly known only as "Dzakutsaku," led by Bishop Muzorewa, until the time he temporarily retired from active politics in 1987, is the focus of this chapter. A number of outstanding politicians of the day have written accounts of those times (Nkomo, Shamuyarira, Smith, Munangagwa, Chambati, Sithole, Banana, and Muzorewa himself). Other helpful literature includes minutes of meetings and press coverage. There is far more than has been published about the reflections of the church leadership at the time, but an attempt has been made to review what does exist (Shiri, Kurewa, Linden, Dodge). There are some crucial details recorded in the small meetings where some national decisions of consequence were hatched.

We have noted earlier that there was a problem of unity among the nationalist movements in Zimbabwe. Most Nationalists had lost focus and were now pursuing only personal gains and positions. There were also leadership struggles within each movement. The liberation of the people of Zimbabwe was no longer the main issue. Africans fighting fellow Africans has existed up to the present day. Everybody wants to be the number one man. Those who had been in detention or even better yet, those who were once imprisoned, felt that they had extra credentials or entitlement to positions of power and special recognition. The detente period of 1974 and 1976 saw attempts to unify Zimbabwe's nationalist movements. In 1974 these efforts resulted in the temporary release from jail of nationalist leaders

The Formation of the United African National Council (1975)

Joshua Nkomo, Robert Mugabe, James Chikerema, and Ndabaningi Sithole for unity talks in Lusaka.[1] The release was granted as a condition for the preparation of a conference between nationalists, Ian Smith and the British government, scheduled for 1975 at Victoria Falls. It is instructive to note that Bishop Muzorewa actually demanded the release of these nationalists as condition for the talks. Ian Smith had no choice.

On December 7, 1974, the major political parties, ZANU, ZAPU, FROLIZI, and the ANC, signed the Lusaka Declaration of Unity to form the new United ANC. Bishop Abel Tendekai Muzorewa became the compromise chairman of the UANC. Dr. Joshua Nkomo, in his autobiography *The Story of My Life*, remarked, "The United-ANC as the compromise body was recognized as the unifying force. Under Muzorewa's chairmanship the presidents of ZAPU, ZANU, and FROLIZI, that is I, Rev. Ndabaningi Sithole, and James Chikerema, with three members of each of the organizations, would form a new executive."[2]

This would be one more opportunity for the leaders to unite with a common purpose. Dr. Nkomo says, "That executive would do any negotiation necessary, with Smith or others. Within four months the executive would also prepare a constitution for a new ANC, and then call a congress to elect a leadership to represent the united people of Zimbabwe."[3]

The congress referred to did not take place. Nkomo blamed Bishop Muzorewa and said his delusions of national leadership were gaining momentum. Nkomo never fully trusted Muzorewa; he simply wanted him to remain an interim figurehead without executive powers. Nkomo began to seriously wonder where the Bishop was getting his mandate to lead the people of the ANC and to increase in the political arena. The key players never trusted his presence, but they wanted to use him when the need arose. Nkomo and other leaders feared that if this congress took place, the people of Zimbabwe, without hesitation, would have endorsed the United-ANC with Bishop Muzorewa as their leader. Power struggles against each other among the three Nationalist Party leaders and within themselves prevented the congress from taking place. That probably saved the nationalist leaders a degree of embarrassment.

Whilst there were struggles in ZAPU and FLORIZI, the worst struggles were within ZANU. My opinion is the ZANU struggles were worsened by the realization that clergy, given a chance to lead, would be selfless and then

1. Shamuyarira, "Overview," 18–19.
2. Nkomo, *Nkomo*, 156.
3. Ibid.

attract more support. The Rev. Ndabaningi Sithole, who was the founding president of ZANU, had to be eliminated before it was too late. Rather than preparing for the congress, the Nationalist leaders who had got a chance to be free from prison were busy setting people at each other's throats. People were divided along ZANU and ZAPU lines. They forgot about the ANC that had served them well and saved the nation from taking the apartheid route that had been planned by Ian Smith. It was this recurring power struggle and internal fighting that convinced the Bishop that his service would continue to be useful.

As a result the United-ANC never saw the light of the day and the Bishop had to follow what the genuine Masses of Zimbabwe were aspiring for—independence.

A conference that might have brought peace in 1975 did not happen. It was arranged to take place on August 25–26, 1975, on the border between Zambia and Rhodesia, on the railway bridge that crosses the Zambezi River at the Victoria Falls, because Smith would not allow the nationalists into Rhodesia without arresting them (they were all classified as dangerous to the country's welfare). Therefore, a white line was drawn across the bridge to mark the exact border, and a train carriage was placed so that its center was exactly on the line, which was then extended so as to bisect a long table running down the middle of the carriage. On the Rhodesian end sat Ian Smith and his teammates P. K Van der Byl, Lardner-Burke, and others. In the nationalist delegation led by Joshua Nkomo were Rev. Ndabaningi Sithole, James Chikerema, and Bishop Muzorewa.[4] Here, even though Bishop Muzorewa had been asked to lead the United-ANC, he gave way to Joshua Nkomo to lead the delegation instead of himself. Although this could have been a perfect occasion for fighting for the number one position, Bishop would not let it be so.

Nkomo noted that the nationalist delegation had clearly agreed that Bishop Muzorewa would do the talking for their side. Later he noted, "He had no experience as a negotiator, and made a real mess of his case: at lunch on the first day it was agreed that Sithole, Chikerema, and I would intervene to support him when he was unable to stand up to Smith's arguments."[5]

Nkomo's statements are questionable. How would Bishop Muzorewa fail to negotiate when he had managed to handle the Pearce Commission so efficiently and convinced both the British and the Americans that the Home-Smith proposals were a bad proposal for the people of Zimbabwe?

4. Ibid., 159.
5. Ibid., 160.

The Formation of the United African National Council (1975)

However, this conference did not achieve any results toward majority rule. Disunity among the nationalist groups dominated the would-be talks. Almost repeatedly, when national unity was at stake, Bishop Muzorewa was the one who was able to restore unity.

Was this a reflection that the Bishop was the only trusted figure within the struggle, or was it that everyone had confidence in a man of the cloth? Or was it a matter of his leadership style?

Interesting events developed soon after the signing of the Lusaka Unity Accord (December 1975). For his part, Joshua Nkomo had set his eyes on the congress stipulated in the unity agreement and hoped to be elected to lead a possibly united movement. Bishop Muzorewa was trying to find his way into ZANLA and ZIPRA military camps in order to introduce himself to the combatants in an effort to consolidate his position as well as serve to unite the two groups.

Emerson D. Munangagwa, who was in the military structures of the nationalist movements at the time, noted that the ANC as a uniting force failed to either assist or stop the war. In October 1975, fighting ZANLA cadres based in Tanzania issued the famous Mgagao Declaration, which was addressed to the OAU's Liberation Committee. The cadres attacked three leaders of the ANC, namely Abel Muzorewa, Ndabaningi Sithole, and James Chikerema, whom they accused of failure to produce the ANC party guidelines; failure to produce machinery capable of prosecuting the war and effecting the armed struggle; failure to arrange for the trained freedom fighters to go and reinforce their colleagues at the front; and failure to make arrangements for the large numbers of recruits in Mozambique to undergo military training.[6]

These issues partially failed because the other Nationalists could not allow the Bishop to meet with the cadres; there was a grant plan to discredit him on that front. If he had managed to meet the cadres and be acceptable to them as a leader, then he was going to be acceptable again to the fighters and the population back home. Those who were self-seeking Nationalists would have lost the game at this point. Hence, the Bishop had to be blocked. However, it can also be noted that two of the three accused were clergymen. How easy was it for the two religious leaders to implement a war plan? How was the Bishop going to handle these demands together with his Episcopal demands? How was he going to relate to church members whose loyalties and interests were on both sides? Could a Bishop actually serve as the Commander-in-Chief? In his role as Bishop, he was the pastor of both sides of

6. Munangagwa, "Formation," 144.

the divided nation. How was he to preach and give orders to kill at the same time? Was he going to commission guerillas to fight, killing some churchgoers who were attending a *sangano* at Nyatande or Chiringaodzi? This is where being the embodiment of church and state becomes very complex. It is especially complicated when neither side was ready to "negotiate," since there was nothing to negotiate at this point. Since it was guerilla warfare, truce was out of the question. Not even the Book of Exodus would help, since the Bishop's situation was more complex than Moses'.

Some analysts note that there were fundamental differences between the Bishop and the other leaders. Apparently, Bishop Muzorewa lost sight of the fact that he was merely a caretaker leader of the United-ANC. Instead, he saw himself as the undisputed substantial leader of ANC whose main role was to act as a spokesman for the umbrella organization with his own peace agenda. He began to advocate for peaceful negotiations with the Smith government and at the same time denouncing the armed struggle. That created an understandable division within the United-ANC.

The Lusaka Declaration of Unity contained an agreement to convene a United-ANC party congress in March 1975. In early 1975, preparations for the congress should have been undertaken, but disputes arose within the UANC. As a result, it was agreed to postpone the congress. Bishop Muzorewa left Rhodesia, invited by the frontline states to a meeting in Dar-es-Salaam in April 1975. After the meeting the Bishop went to Mozambique to join the camps. While in Mozambique the Bishop announced that he had expelled Joshua Nkomo, the leader of ZAPU, from the UANC. Joshua Nkomo dismissed Bishop Muzorewa's action as being "foolish and childish."[7] The Bishop was now in a power struggle to control the ANC. Whether he was still a Nationalist novice or a veteran would remain to be seen.

The Bishop also made a visit to ZANLA guerilla camps to test his acceptability to them as their leader, but he was rejected by the guerillas. The groundwork to have him rejected had already been prepared by the ideology that Jesus was a white man, and this was the white man Muzorewa worshipped. It is important to note that at this time also Rev. Ndabaningi Sithole was being pushed out of ZANU's leadership. More and more emphasis on ancestrology created a degree of resentment for the clergymen.

Ariston Chambati, who was in the leadership of FROLIZI during the United-ANC days, made the observation,

---

7. Chambati, "National Unity-ANC," 156.

The Formation of the United African National Council (1975)

Following these developments, the majority of the members of the UANC had lost confidence in their leader. They called for a congress at which new leaders could be elected. Interestingly, some leaders who were loyal to Bishop Muzorewa began disassociating themselves from the majority of members. There was certainly a clear division within the UANC in the country between those who supported Joshua Nkomo and those who belonged to Bishop Muzorewa. Consequently, two organizations emerged.[8]

These developments indicate that ZANU never got into the United-ANC; hence, the ball was left with Nkomo of ZAPU and Muzorewa while ZANU was simply consolidating positions of power and control of the armed forces to survive what was coming. This use of and reliance on the armed forces has existed up to the present day. The fighters were urged to ignore Nkomo and Muzorewa, and that is how ZIPA died; ZANLA was never integrated fully. The politics of the gun took root. Even at independence, ZANLA was never fully integrated. A separate army, Gukurahundi, was formed and used to crush ZAPU.

The Bishop was now part of the conflict between the nationalist African leaders. He had been elected in Zambia as a uniting figure, but now he was at the center of the conflict without effective control of the situation. Thus, the ANC umbrella was divided into two camps, a development of great concern to the frontline states, which, in an effort to heal the split, called for a meeting in Dar-es-Salaam. The big question at this point was, What was the Bishop's focus? Was it personal power or resolving the national conflict or majority rule at home? My opinion is that since the Bishop had tasted power and now he was getting into the power struggles, the boys (Vakomana) had pushed him into the corner and he had to do what was expedient to survive.

The Dar-es-Salaam meeting failed to achieve unity among the four nationalist leaders. The frontline leaders then diverted their energy toward attempting to unite the liberation movements—ZANU and ZAPU—and their efforts culminated in the formation of the Patriotic Front in October 1976.[9] The Bishop should have been able to read the meaning of this change from the frontline states. He was no longer the clear representative of the armed liberation movements of the people of Zimbabwe. Whilst the ANC was concentrating on uniting the people on the ground, those in ZANU were mostly working on the frontline states and the armed guerrillas. ZAPU survived because Nkomo was known as the founder of Nationalism in Rhodesia by

8. Ibid.
9. Ibid, 156–57.

the frontline states leaders. Hence, they would always look for him in every puzzle. This always infuriated Mugabe. This is also the time a coup took place in ZANU. Ndabaningi Sithole was displaced by a nonreligious leader. It was clearly the aim of the nationalists to do away with religious leaders and go on the warpath. Does this indicate the impossibility of the compatibility of church and state? Or does it suggest that the two can interact and are not necessarily exclusive?

7

United African National Council, the Bishop's Own Path

THE LUSAKA ACCORD AND the subsequent recognition of the ANC by the Council of OAU ministers was, indeed, the peak of UANC's performance toward resolving the national problem. However, there was a serious split within the ZANU membership of the UANC over the acceptability of Rev Ndabaningi Sithole as president of ZANU. After the assassination of Herbert Chitepo in Lusaka in March 1975, Robert Mugabe and Edgar Tekere had emerged from within Rhodesia as new leaders of the ZANU party. These new leaders did not feel bound by the Lusaka Agreement with Bishop Muzorewa claiming control over its military wing. One immediate problem for the UANC leadership was therefore how it could prove its control of the military wings of ZANU and ZAPU. In spite of the resistance within the respective parties, Muzorewa and Sithole persisted in their view of their role and authority toward the liberation armies. In August 1975, they formed the ANC-Zimbabwe Liberation Council, or ANC-Z, as an expression of their claims. This was to be the ANC war council.

To add to the confusion, Nkomo seems to reflect that he gave Muzorewa permission to be the Commander-in-Chief of the ZIPRA forces, writing,

> The Bishop had no army at all, but while he was acting as interim President of the ANC that we had agreed to set up at Lusaka, I allowed him the title of Commander-in-Chief of ZIPRA. It was during this period that he visited some of my soldiers in Zambia, and someone gave him a light machine gun to look at: he was photographed waving this thing around, and so was born the dream

of Muzorewa, the great jungle fighter. The Bishop's supporters invented the slogan "Heavy-Heavy" *(dzakutsaku)*, referring to the time when he had trouble lifting the sub-machine gun and implying that he was the leader of many armed soldiers.[1]

Given the events taking place in the ANC, how did this affect the church in general? It is interesting to compare the impressions of clergy enrolled in seminary in 1976 at the United Theological (Protestant) College at Epworth, Harare, with similar assessments of the atmosphere at Chishawasha Regional (Catholic) Seminary, Harare. At the time of the split of ANC, both had distinguished African theologians and churchmen at the helm. At Epworth, the Rev. Dr. C. Mazobere became the first African Principal of United Theological College (UTC). At Chishawasha in 1976, Fr. Tobias Chigiya was promoted and become the first African Rector of the Seminary.[2] Reporting from a pastoral visit to UTC at Epworth in October 1976, C. Manyoba of the Methodist Church shared the following impressions: "The recent build-up for the Geneva Conference has increased the tension among the theological students at UTC, and there are differences following the lines of the African political camps."[3] When he ventured an assessment of the support of the different factions among the students, Manyoba said, "The section which is strong numerically is that supporting the Bishop's ANC." He had also heard that lately this group had started organizing prayer meetings for Geneva (an all-parties constitutional conference to resolve the Rhodesia problem, held in Geneva, Switzerland, in 1975) at their own times, without the permission and authority of the principal. Meanwhile he reported that the Catholic students at Chishawasha were strongly in favor of ZANU and Mugabe, who is reported to be Roman Catholic.[4]

There also arose a situation in Harare's townships where members of the same church congregation were divided along political lines. The Rev. Andrew Ndhlela, who was the President of the Methodist Church Synod, was concerned with the split in the ANC, and he made the following statement to the synod delegates in 1975: "It is unfortunate and disappointing that there arose a split within the ANC organization. Many of the followers do not know the reasons why there is this split. Both Africans and Europeans hope that there are going to be negotiations leading to settlement."[5]

1. Nkomo, *Nkomo*, 161, 163.
2. Hellencreutz, *Religion and Politics*, 425.
3. Ibid., 426.
4. Ibid., 427.
5. Ibid., 428.

Expressing his own opinion, Ndhela said, "I would like to state quite clearly that the Church should not take part in the split. The Church should not be put in that situation. Each individual can support one of the ANC factions if he so wishes. The negotiations with the government are taking place with one faction of the ANC."[6]

As the national President of the Methodist Church, Ndhlela, decreed,

> On behalf of the African people and the church, I call upon all leaders of both ANC factions to come together and fight the settlement-battle—it is not too late. I am not optimistic of a settlement arising from the talks which are presently continuing, but I say that even if the talks will not produce a settlement, talks should continue until a settlement is achieved without bloodshed.[7]

These references show the extent to which political developments were considered openly as part of the churches' legitimate agenda. On the part of other religious leaders, the Christian Council of Rhodesia (CCR 1975) took an initiative that could easily be interpreted as evidence of direct support for the cause of Bishop Muzorewa. In 1973 the Smith government had banned The United Methodist Church periodical, UMBOWO.[8] Fortunately, the literature committee of the CCR recommended taking over editorial responsibilities for UMBOWO and developing it into an ecumenical newspaper. On November 13, 1975, the CCR appointed Richard Chikosi as editor of the new ecumenical UMBOWO, thereby circumventing the ban effect of this informative periodical.[9]

Richard Chikosi was an enterprising and committed journalist involved in the search for the liberation of Zimbabwe. He was aware that the political stand of UMBOWO had been decided already in 1971, "when the head of The United Methodist Church in Rhodesia had become Rhodesia's black nationalist leader."[10] Chikosi thus defined his task as a "continuation of an already established Christian stand on the national struggle for majority rule, which had the blessing of virtually all Christians in and outside the

---

6. Ibid.

7. Ibid.

8. Muzorewa, *Rise Up and Walk*, 189.

9. CCR Executive Committee, February 18 and April 8, 1975, and the CCR Council meeting November 13, 1976.

10. Editor's report, January–December 1976, presented to CCR Annual Meeting, April 1977.

country and the approval of the greater majority of members of the Christian Council of Rhodesia."[11]

Chikosi's political preferences are quite apparent in Umbowo. For example, the issue for the October–November 1976 issue focused on the return to Zimbabwe of Bishop Muzorewa from his exile in Mozambique. Bishop Muzorewa was revered as the "Moses of Zimbabwe." Photographs in UMBOWO from the mass rally in Highfields of October 3, 1976, illustrate that the UANC at the time still had a strong grassroots base.[12] In his autobiography, Bishop Muzorewa admits that this tremendous welcome home, as reported in Umbowo, inspired his participation later in the Geneva talks.[13] The Bishop took these publicized gestures as a mandate from the people to continue in the political arena in order to liberate the populace.

Meanwhile Ian Smith was closely monitoring the situation in the UANC. When things began to change, he labeled Bishop Muzorewa an inexperienced politician. Smith wrote, "Muzorewa was caught in the middle: he supported the agreement with us but lacked experience and political acumen. The old seasoned leaders were able to mould him to their wishes."[14] Of interest is that from this moment in 1975 on, Smith never addressed Muzorewa as Bishop but simply "Muzorewa," as if to suggest that he had surrendered his Episcopal office for politics. Smith observed that Muzorewa could carry a gun if that was the right thing to do, and he could carry the Bible without feeling any contradiction, since there was none.

Smith interprets the UANC unity under Bishop Muzorewa as a result of pressure from the frontline states. His intelligence reports told him that any attempt to unite the two factions (ZANU and ZAPU) under Bishop Muzorewa and the UANC had no chance of succeeding and would be purely superficial.[15] This gave Smith the opportunity to scheme his plan for an internal settlement with Muzorewa and Sithole, who by now were no longer wanted as leaders in the UANC. The nationalists no longer wanted clergymen leading the liberation movements since they were now seriously leaning toward a full-fledged armed struggle. It is possible that the nationalists recognized a contradiction in roles between church leadership and military leadership. But it is also likely that it was a matter of morals. The clergymen

---

11. Ibid.
12. Umbowo, October–November 1976.
13. Muzorewa, *Rise Up and Walk*, 210–13.
14. Smith, *Bitter Harvest*, 165.
15. Ibid., 165, 177.

had seen how ruthless the nationalists could be with each other. Advocate Herbert Chitepo's assassination was a case in point.

Smith notes that in 1976 a man called Gabellah, who claimed to lead the ANC in Matebeleland, reported to him that he had had a few meetings with Muzorewa in Malawi and found him on the horns of a dilemma. Bishop Muzorewa, intrinsically a peaceful man, was hoping for a peaceful settlement. However, under the influence of Sithole, he had become a supporter of what Smith termed "terrorism." Thus, according to Smith's interpretation, he had acquired a dual personality, was disillusioned, and was unable to make up his mind. It is interesting that Smith also noted, concerning the division in ZANU between ethnic groups (Karangas and Manyikas), that Bishop Muzorewa was acceptable to both groups.[16] Thus, Smith began to perceive that Bishop Muzorewa was truly a peace-loving man, even when the odds were great.

---

16. Ibid., 190.

8

Internal Settlement or Intensified War: The Bishop Chooses

THE BREAKDOWN OF THE Unity Accord from Lusaka in December 1974, the split of the ANC, and the formation of the Patriotic Front (PF) as a new expression of the shared concerns of the Zimbabwean Liberation Forces inspired James Callaghan of the new Labor Government to activate British diplomacy in a renewed attempt to establish peace and legitimacy in Zimbabwe. This paved the way for a constitutional conference in Geneva, which began on October 26, 1976. Under pressure, Ian Smith realized that he had to attend.

The liberation movements, ZANU and ZAPU, went together to Geneva under the newly formed Patriotic Front (PF). Bishop Muzorewa called this event a "do-nothing conference."[1] Things went wrong when the Patriotic Front withdrew their support for new peace proposals because they feared that Bishop Muzorewa, now leading the UANC or United ANC as a separate political entity, might be trying to hijack their positions as top leaders of the nationalist movement.

Apparently at Geneva the freedom of the people was no longer a priority in the nationalist discussion but rather on personal power and gain as the end of white rule was imminent. The PF leadership of Robert Mugabe and Jason Moyo simply withdrew from Geneva because Bishop Muzorewa was beginning to be recognized as the leader of the UANC and as such the recognized leader of the Zimbabwean people. The Bishop could have opened up the way for these leaders who were pushing to be recognized since they had

---

1. Mitchell, *In Search of Freedom*, 44.

been in from detention and exile. Alternatively, he could have entered into an alliance with them. But each leader was looking first and foremost after his own position. So was the Bishop. This was one of the main reasons for the long delays in the nationalist struggle reaching any successful conclusion and the cause of despair among the other peace-loving nationalists who only had the objective of majority rule.

Meanwhile, viewing the Geneva event from the angle of the churches, it is notable that in all the delegations from Zimbabwe, there were churchmen involved. Josiah Chinamano was a Methodist lay preacher and Garfield Todd was a former missionary of the Church of Christ. Joshua Nkomo himself was a lay preacher in the Methodist Church. These three were members of the PF-ZAPU team. The Rev. Canaan Banana was released from prison and took part in Bishop Muzorewa's UANC delegation. There was also Stanlake Samkange, a lay pastor who had made a comeback in Rhodesian politics after his academic career in the United States. Nathan Shamuyarira, who was a member of the Methodist Synod, was part of Robert Mugabe's ZANU-PF delegation. The Rev. N. Sithole of the United Church of Christ headed the delegation from his own ZANU. As the meeting took place in Geneva, the World Council of Churches, through its Program to Combat Racism, was ready to provide certain assistance to the African delegation.[2] The merging of church and political interests as evidenced by this lineup of people present at the Geneva conference is an extraordinary development in the modern history of the global church. Again, the church and state dichotomy is not all that dichotomous when millions of people are suffering oppression and being dehumanized. This is where Jesus's question can be instructive: If an ox is stuck in the mud on a Sabbath, is it lawful to rescue it?

The constitutional conference in Geneva was a significant opportunity for the African political leaders to meet and state the position of their respective parties. There was, however, too great a divergence of views between the different African positions, and even more so between these and those of Ian Smith. The negotiations soon reached a standstill. Parallel to the formal negotiations, there were secret talks between Ian Smith and Bishop Muzorewa about the terms for a possible internal settlement without the involvement of the Patriotic Front. These discussions took place against the advice of Reverend Banana, who had accompanied the Bishop, and when he heard of them he responded by crossing the floor to become part of Robert Mugabe's delegation.[3]

2. Hellencreutz, *Religion and Politics*, 432.
3. Ibid.

Religious Leadership in National Political Conflicts

For this move to join Mugabe the Rev. Canaan Banana was eventually rewarded. He became the nominal head of state at Independence. He was later pushed before his term came to end when Mugabe wanted to be the executive president and consolidate his power. Some also suggested that because of Rev. Canaan Banana's UANC and Muzorewa background he would not be buried at the National Heroes acre when he finally died. But there might have been other social reasons. However, it is unthinkable that the first president would be denied the honor.

Hopes and prayers in different churches in Rhodesia followed the Geneva Conference. Vice President of the Christian Council of Rhodesia Reverend Andrew Ndhlela took part in an informal delegation to Geneva, a trip sponsored by Zimbabwe's Heads of Denominations. Addressing his synod soon after his return from the Geneva conference, he shared his views of the significance of the exercise: "I went to Geneva because of the seriousness of the situation. . . . The nationalists want nothing less than African majority rule and handover of power. I tried to bring them the spirit of give-and-take and reconciliation."[4]

This leader of the Methodist Church, sent by the heads of most denominations in Zimbabwe, took a bold decision to provide a pastoral service at the conference. He met with the leaders of the liberation movements. The wider church leadership took a very important non-political position; a positive and persuasive role to see to it that the national conflict was resolved. They did not wait to be invited; they sent their own delegate to the Geneva Conference to negotiate in the background for certain principles rather than party interests. The Rev. Andrew Ndhlela boldly advised all the groups that war was not in the interests of the people at home, but they wanted a peaceful settlement without loss of life. It is significant that Zimbabwe's Heads of Denominations found it necessary to send their own delegation to Geneva to carry out this pastoral mission despite the fact that one of their own number, Bishop Muzorewa, and several other clergy and lay leaders were present in the political party delegations. Heads of denominations felt that a non-partisan voice might be heard since the clergy, who were already there, represented their own ground. At this point, Bishop Muzorewa was no longer viewed as the uniting force since he was representing a particular political faction. Was this time for him to quit?

After the breakdown of the talks in December 1976, Bishop Muzorewa was faced with three possible options: either to withdraw from politics and dissolve his party, align himself with the Patriotic Front under Mugabe and

4. Ibid.

Internal Settlement or Intensified War: The Bishop Chooses

Nkomo, or to embark on a road toward an internal settlement with Ian Smith. During the Geneva Conference the Rev. Canaan Banana had already opted for the second alternative. The events within the UANC at Geneva 1976 thus made evident theological and ideological differences between Bishop Muzorewa and Rev. Banana, which may have been reinforced by Banana's more direct espousal during his studies in the United States of radical Latin-American liberation theology allowing for a "just war" approach to overthrowing oppressive political domination.

Withdrawing from politics was not the Bishop's choice. He chose the third option, to negotiate with Smith at a time when the Patriotic Front stepped up the war. The bishop first indicated publicly that he was ready to involve himself in negotiations with Smith in August, just before he went to London for discussions with Owen, the British Foreign Secretary, in 1977.[5] He returned to Salisbury to find his party organization disintegrating due to disagreement over negotiating with Smith. He dissolved the Central Committee of the UANC and appointed a replacement committee including three more clergymen of varying denominations: Rev. Maxwell Chigwida, Rev. Dr. John W. Z. Kurewa, and Rev. T. Kadonhera.[6]

In his autobiography, Bishop Muzorewa expresses his initial anxieties about Smith's initiative. Talking to Smith at that time was considered political suicide. There were similar problems to siding himself with the other invitees to the internal settlement discussions. Did Bishop Muzorewa want to associate himself with Chief Chirau and the Rev. Ndabaningi Sithole? In his book, the Bishop looks back to that moment and writes,

> There did not appear to be alternatives. The war was raging, taking scores of lives every week. Our people were a pathetic sight. There was massive unemployment. Hundreds of thousands of the people were living in camps, virtually refugees in their own country. The economy of the country was on the brink of collapse. What frightened me most and worried me sick was that the black population looked to me to do something about the situation. The faith of the people in me was one of the heaviest crosses I have ever carried. I had to keep on trying and my worries were torture.[7]

This is one of the Bishop's political responsibilities described in terms of his spiritual vocation. The expectation of the people he refers to could

---

5. *The Rhodesia Herald*, August 8, 1977.
6. *The Rhodesia Herald*, August 25, 1977.
7. Muzorewa, *Rise Up and Walk*, 226.

have been coming from 1972, when he saved the people from the Homes proposals during the Pearce Commission. It could also be a reference to the hearty welcome by crowds in October 1976 as he returned to Harare from Mozambique, or to a number of individuals and groups who pressed him into taking political action. The Bishop seems to have been under pressure. He had to do something, so he opted to negotiate with Smith. What Bishop Muzorewa does not convey in his autobiography is the content of the package Smith was promising and offering to him that influenced his decision. Did he enforce modifications to Smith's racist policies prior to and after Geneva 1976? Nor does he explain how his own decisions relate to the crisis apparent in his own party. What we know is that the Bishop wanted to minimize bloodshed in this whole exercise. As a parent, it was his son fighting as a guerilla, his other son fighting in the Rhodesian army, and his mother caged in the various camps! This was the dilemma the Bishop faced.

It is interesting that Joshua Nkomo echoes Bishop Muzorewa's thinking about the need to stop the war:

> The last and bitterest stages of the Zimbabwe liberation war were entirely unnecessary. By 1977 Ian Smith's regime was doomed. Politically, he tried to set up an internal deal, which would preserve the power of the white minority but give his friends in the outside world some justification for claiming that Rhodesia was now multiracial and could therefore be recognized. Smith chose Bishop Muzorewa, and also maneuvered into his corner the more significant figure of Rev. Ndabaningi Sithole, "who was bitter at the way he had been ousted from the leadership of ZANU." He added chiefs Chirau and Ndiweni, salaried employees of the government. Smith's multiracial charade would look acceptable.[8]

Given Nkomo's observations and Bishop Muzorewa's remarks it shows that the most terrible years of the war could have been avoided had it not been for the power struggles within the leadership of the African nationalists themselves.

A survey of Catholic approaches to these events is instructive. Throughout the war the Catholic Commission on Justice and Peace consistently drew attention to human rights violations by the security forces, often to the anger of the more prosperous white Catholic laity in the towns. During this period Catholic bishops issued no less than thirteen pastoral instructions, and these were titled "A Plea for Peace" (1965), "A Call to Christians" (1969), "Reconciliation in Rhodesia" (1974), and "A Plea for Reconciliation"

---

8. Nkomo, *Nkomo*, 193.

(1978).⁹ Catholic Bishop Lamont of the Mutare Diocese was not a left-wing liberation theologian but very much in the conservative wing of the Catholic Church. He had studied in Rome at the height of the Fascist era in the 1930s, and what he saw happening toward the end of his thirty years' ministry in Rhodesia reminded him of the events in Europe in a previous generation. In October 1976 he was sentenced to ten years in prison for failing to report the presence of guerrillas and of telling others to do likewise. In the following year, at the age of sixty-five, he was stripped of his citizenship and deported after a trial in which both his statement and the judgment against him made by Chief Justice MacDonald were overtly political in content.[10]

A Jesuit priest, Fidelis Mukonori, who was Vice Chairman of the Catholic Justice and Peace Commission during part of the war, taught leadership courses for the Catholic youth. This made him a familiar figure to groups throughout the country. His teaching included claims that not to fight against the dehumanizing effects of racism was a sin against the Holy Spirit. Dehumanizing people makes them less than the temple and image of God; all human beings were called to live a dignified life. At a time when large numbers of youth were crossing the borders to join the guerilla bases in neighboring countries, his teaching showed young freedom fighters that Christian principles were to be respected. He traveled secretly throughout the war zones and to guerilla camps in Mozambique and attended the all-night meetings, *pungwes*, where the guerrillas would teach the populace about their objectives.[11] It was possible to teach Christian principles to the fighters, to respect human dignity and human values. Without a way to evaluate the impact of such teaching, at least one can guess that Christianity and traditional religion played a role in the liberation war.

A number of other Catholic missionaries made the decision to live among the guerillas for non-combat service. These included Fr. Nigel Johnson, a Jesuit who lived with ZIPRA forces in Zambia, and Sister Janice McLaughlin, a Maryknoll sister living with ZANLA forces in Tanzania and Mozambique after the Smith government expelled her from Rhodesia for her "terrorist" sympathies.[12] Dominican Sister Mary Aquina helped to smuggle support out of Zimbabwe to the ZANLA forces until she was apprehended and left the country under threat of arrest. Bishop Patrick Mutume was constantly in touch with the guerillas and was put on trial to face the death

9. Randolph, *Dawn in Zimbabwe*, chap. 12.
10. De Waal, *Politics of Reconciliation*, 62.
11. British Council of Churches, *Violence in Southern Africa*, 73, 76–77.
12. McLaughlin, *On the Frontline*, 61–63.

penalty for this reason. He has up to the present day remained a voice of the people of Zimbabwe in search for unity. In recent years he led a delegation of three bishops from Manicaland to discuss unity of purpose with Robert Mugabe and Morgan Tsvangirai. This was the first initiative to bring the two leaders together that eventually progressed to the signing of the GNU. The ushering in of the Unity Government that relieved the people of Zimbabwe is a product of this initiative. Most Catholic missions were heavily engaged with the liberation forces, either by force or by choice, due to their locations along the border. This gave the Catholic Church a much closer alignment with ZANU and ZAPU's military approach to solve the Rhodesian problem. In addition, Catholic communities were directly using Latin American liberation theology, which takes a community approach, throughout the war. Animate local resistance to the Smith regime CCJP would reflect this, although they were carefully guarded to avoid repercussions from the Rhodesia government. In sum, the Catholics did not have an ethical problem with engaging in war while in religious garb if it was a liberation war.

From 1977 onward the official Roman Catholic position on church-state relations had a sharper profile than that of the CCR, which appeared to have shifted its focus from the political level to the humanitarian level. Reports of the effects of the war in different parts of the country became more frequent in CCR's deliberations.[13] Racial injustices, unemployment, and other war-induced "sufferings of our people throughout the country" were major causes of concern in the CCR and formed the basis of their political considerations more overtly than the objective of majority rule. In an extraordinarily detailed report to the annual meeting of 1978, CCR General Secretary Watyoka summarized the analysis of the Council and its political conclusions: "I beg to remind us of what we have consistently urged and prayed for during the year as we considered the suffering of our people throughout the country. We sought justice, peace and a new opportunity to live a full life."[14]

Watyoka continued to itemize concerns: "We called for the removal of the causes of war by establishing rule of justice under a government of the people. We said that nothing less than a universal franchise would satisfy today's demand to share in government."[15]

---

13. CCR Executive Committee, April 19, and Council Meeting, April 20.
14. CCR General Secretary's report, 1978 Annual Meeting.
15. Ibid.

To conclude, the General Secretary said, "We called for an end of such executions, release of detainees and political prisoners, and an end to putting people into so-called protected villages and an end to all racial segregation."[16]

However, the immediate political conclusion that the majority of the council drew in 1977 was to endorse internal settlement negotiation. After all, Bishop Muzorewa was still a member of the CCR.[17] As a veteran politician, Percy M'kundu, who was CCR's president, had always opted for parliamentary measures as a means of achieving national liberation and improved social conditions. After the formation of UANC, M'kundu made a political comeback, being appointed a member of the National Executive Committee of UANC.[18] As a body the members of the CCR were convinced that the nonviolent approach to the Rhodesian conflict was the way to go, although there may have been differences among individual heads of denominations, as with the Catholic bishops. When Bishop Muzorewa started the internal negotiations, he seemed to have support from many Christian leaders in the country.

Professor Emeritus Marshall Murphree of the Center for Applied Social Sciences in the University of Zimbabwe recalls that toward dawn on Easter Day 1976, in the Eastern Highlands in Manicaland, he and his wife were in the congregation of a Methodist Church that had gathered in the open for the traditional sunrise service. The people were looking east, waiting for the sun-symbol of new life, of Christ who and is coming among them. As the congregation prayed and sang, Professor Murphree gradually became aware that they were looking eastward to Mozambique, and were in fact looking for their children who were coming to liberate them. He remembers saying to his wife, "Smith has lost the war; the parents have gone over to the freedom fighters."[19] Clearly it is possible to be critical of the aims and conduct of both sides in a dispute, and that is what the Rhodesian churches had tried to do in the years leading up to the guerrilla war. And during the war it seemed there were much to criticize and much to condemn. Of course, it goes without saying that the church abhorred intimidation and murder by the guerrillas, but they were equally forthright in noting and condemning

---

16. Ibid.

17. CCR Annual meeting, April 20, 1977.

18. *The Rhodesia Herald*, October 14, 1977. Cf. Chikosi's report on the period during the General Secretary's absence, November 2, 1977.

19. De Waal, *Politics of Reconciliation*, 58.

the excesses of Smith's security forces.[20] Truly, people were caught between a rock and a hard place. But one thing was clear: they wanted their freedom.

It is of interest to note the stance of the Anglican Church throughout these times given that they had the largest white population, which was more (although by no means entirely) inclined to have relatives fighting Smith's army. No Anglican Episcopal voice was heard criticizing Smith's forces until 1976 when Bishop Murindagomo, the first black suffrage bishop, was moved to oppose his superior, Bishop Paul Burrough of Mashonaland: "The longing for a just society is causing revolutions all over the world."

Murindagomo added:

> Since many Christians are deeply rooted in the status quo, they tend primarily to be concerned with the maintenance of law and order, understandably, but where the maintenance of order is an obstacle to a just order, some will decide for revolutionary action against that injustice, struggling for a just society without which the new humanity cannot fully come.[21]

Neutrality was not an option for the Christian communities in the rural areas who lived in midst of the guerrilla war. For all the ambiguities of the situation in which they found themselves, they had to choose whether to support the freedom fighters in their overall objectives. Such a choice was not easy either. If one condemned guerrillas in favor of Smith's army, that would result in a fatality or serious mutilation.

Many church leaders, both clergy and laity, lost their lives during the war. In fact, anybody who held a position of leadership, especially in the communal lands, was liable to face death at any time. Professor Kurewa says, "I recall attending a funeral of a United Methodist Pastor and his wife, Elisha and Tamary Kuwana, who had both been brutally murdered by the Rhodesian Security Forces at Chitenderano. . . . On another occasion I confronted the security forces after they shot a young United Methodist pastor, Thomas Mvenge, who was trying to stop some of the government security forces from aimlessly beating people in a 'keep.' Indeed, it was a rule of terror."[22] I remember how the Kuwanas were killed very well. It was getting dark when we heard the two gun shots. These were the first gun shots I ever heard in my life; from then on it was a daily routine in the village. Every now and then people were running away from gun fires and battle rages between Rhode-

---

20. Ibid., 60.
21. Lapsley, *Neutrality or Co-option*, 55.
22. Kurewa, *Church in Mission*, 156.

sian forces and the freedom fighters. Life could not go on like that. Yet when leaders sat at the negotiating table, priority was given to who got what key position. One wonders what role prayer played in all this.

These are signs of a cross-denominational religious leadership who were at the center of the conflict and making efforts to resolve it. Bishop Muzorewa's chosen role was therefore not out of step with the times and cannot be evaluated as an insulated and isolated personal agenda. Indeed, he was one among many churchmen who made their contribution to the liberation struggle. His prominence arose from recognition of his oratory talent and his professional history in the SCM, which placed him into a more public role nationally. The fact that he had become the first black bishop in Zimbabwe increased both his visibility and public responsibility. Nevertheless, it also caused him much inward dilemma as he tried to balance ecclesial and political responsibilities, both of which addressed the question of millions of souls.

How was African nationalism understood and interpreted by the church in Africa? Most people in Africa would have no problem answering this question, for everyone has experienced nationalism in one way or the other and could very easily identify with the manifestation of its spirit. As Robert Rotberg writes, "In spite of all the obvious manifestations of nationalism, its spirit remains, like most spirits, capable only of inexact description. It is, in essence, pretty much what it is."[23]

This is indeed the way in which the church in Africa came to understand the spirit of African Nationalism; it came to grips with it only as it manifested itself. Alan Paton, a great Christian spokesman of South Africa, in his paper to the All-Africa Conference of Churches at Ibadan in 1958 made the point that African nationalism was inevitable in all its manifestations. At its best, he saw it as self-respect and integrity in a person; at its worst, he perceived it as arrogance, selfishness, and even cruelty in a person. Dr. K. A. Busia of the Ghana Christian Council interpreted African nationalism primarily as a demand for racial equality—Africans demanding acceptance as equals in the human family.[24]

Reverend Ndabaningi Sithole saw many new elements in African nationalism: a new approach to problems facing the African, a new way of removing other-determination and establish self-determination. The church in Africa in general, and in Zimbabwe in particular, has taken African

---

23. Ibid., 113.
24. Ibid., 114.

nationalism seriously.[25] African nationalism was also best expressed in the all Africa national anthem: "*Mwari Komborerai Africa*" (God Bless Africa), meaning that with God's blessing on the continent there will be no more suffering, poverty, oppression, greed, corruption, racism, or selfishness. We will operate as a big family.

As noted earlier in this book, in 1963 at Kampala, the All-Africa Conference of Churches made a significant statement about African nationalism and defined it as "the common desire of a people to work together for their emancipation from any form of bondage, whether colonial, economic, social, or racial."[26]

---

25. Ndabaningi interview.
26. All Africa Conference of Churches, *Drumbeats from Kampala*, 60.

9

Zimbabwe-Rhodesia

AFTER GENEVA, OTHER CONFERENCES were held in Malta in the Mediterranean and in Dar-es-Salaam, Tanzania, as an attempt to resolve the Rhodesian crisis. These again failed to reach any agreement. Ian Smith made final preparations for his internal settlement, continuing to woo Bishop Muzorewa and UANC and Rev. Ndabaningi Sithole's ZANU Mwenje, as well as Chief Chirau of Mashonaland and Chief Ndiweni of Matebeleland. By now Bishop Muzorewa realized that Joshua Nkomo and Robert Mugabe in the Patriotic Front had their own plans and were determined to squeeze him out.[1] The Bishop believed in a nonviolent approach, and Smith capitalized on that orientation—in fact, he took advantage of it.

However, according to Smith, Bishop Muzorewa was the difficult man during the internal negotiations; he was more of a hard-liner than Rev. Sithole and Chiefs Chirau and Ndiweni. Smith notes, "It was obvious to me that if either Muzorewa or Sithole walked out completely, this would play into the hands of the British and their terrorist protégés. On February 7, 1978, Muzorewa asked to withdraw and pray for the people who were being killed by the Rhodesian Forces."[2] Here the Bishop was making a point to the Smith delegation on the internal settlement talks. Even by the time the agreement was to be signed, Smith noted that "the Bishop was not ready to sign but was pressured."[3] Finally, "on March 2, 1978, after a great deal of maneuvering, cajoling and threatening, the rest of the participants succeeded

---

1. Mitchell, *In Search of Freedom*, 42.
2. Smith, *Bitter Harvest*, 246.
3. Ibid.

in getting Muzorewa into the starting stalls, and a public announcement was made that evening that a signing ceremony would be held the following morning."[4] The Bishop's remark to the press that night, "I am in the mood for signing," is questionable.

Apparently Bishop Muzorewa made his decision to sign without adequate consultation with his party structures. When the Bishop went away to Britain and the United States to promote this internal settlement, his Cabinet in the UANC wanted to oust him because they were not comfortable with it. Again we see here a clash of interest between the Bishop's personal and ethical urging and the expectations of his political constituency. Could it be that these are instances when the Bishop would choose God's voice rather than man's wishes? Or else why would he go it alone when his usual style was consultation? Maybe we will never know.

Smith hoped that he could use Muzorewa's church strength in the United States to push for the recognition of their settlement by the U.S. Government. He wrote, "For some months I had been working on an idea of using Bishop Muzorewa and Rev. Sithole through their university and church connections in the USA to organize a visit by the Executive Council to explain to responsible American opinion the justification of our case."[5] But Smith continued to call Muzorewa a weak leader. He actually said, "Our black people were now paying the price for using him as a respectable front for their campaign in 1972 to reject the agreement I had made with Alec Home. After they had succeeded in this exercise, there had been attempts to move him aside, but he had successfully resisted these, so they were hoisted by their own petard."[6]

The churches took different positions with regard to the internal settlement. In August 1978, Archbishop Chakaipa headed an official delegation of the Catholic Church (they were not members of the CCR) that went to Lusaka for discussions with the Patriotic Front.[7] The CCR was at first prepared to side with Bishop Muzorewa and give the internal settlement a try. Even so, there were those who had reservations: Garfield Todd of Dadaya Mission, who was a liberal white former Rhodesian Prime Minister and sympathetic to the cause of majority rule, was an early critic of the internal settlement.[8]

4. Ibid., 247.
5. Ibid., 269.
6. Ibid., 279.
7. Linden, *Church and State*, 275–80.
8. Hellencreutz, *Religion and Politics*, 439.

In spite of the implied criticism of security forces in some reports from the local parishes and mission districts in eastern Zimbabwe, Anglican Bishop Burrough, whose congregations included white Rhodesians with family members fighting in Smith's forces against the Patriotic Front, went on record as a staunch supporter of the internal settlement. In addition to his statement in the diocesan periodical *The Link* in April 1978, Burrough informed his colleagues in the church that even if there were tremendous questions hanging over Rhodesia, he found no need for pessimism, for he believed that on the basis of the internal settlement a democratically elected African government was likely to be in power in 1979. From then on improvements would take place, though not as rapidly as people believed.[9]

The implication here is that the nationalist guerillas would lose out. This explicit support for the internal settlement was reiterated when Bishop Burrough's diocesan standing committee met in September to attend to the issue of the Programme to Combat Racism (PCR), a humanitarian program initiated by the World Council of Churches (WCC) to support people affected by racism. In Rhodesia, PCR's services took the form of humanitarian support for refugees being cared for in ZANLA and ZIPRA camps. The immediate reason for the new discussion on the Programme to Combat Racism was the decision of the WCC to continue its grants to ZANU and ZAPU for refugee care and to terminate its support to Bishop Muzorewa's UANC after the signing of the March 3 agreement. Bishop Burrough's diocesan committee decided not to pay its annual contributions to the WCC because of this very political reason.[10]

Ian Smith's defeat on the issue of black majority rule came not at the hands of Britain or America "We could defy them as we had done over the years"—but at those of South Africa. Their prime minister, John Vorster, thought that after the Portuguese withdrew from its southern African colonies in 1974 a deal would have to be struck with the black states to the north. Thus the internal settlement of 1978 with those black leaders, but predominantly with Bishop Muzorewa, who had remained at liberty in the country and was willing to compromise, was pushed by the apartheid regime in South Africa. The settlement and the elections that followed, as a result of which Muzorewa became the Prime Minister of "Zimbabwe-Rhodesia,"

---

9. Quoted from National Archives of Zimbabwe, file ms.1936/10.6. Minutes: Diocesan standing committee, May 13, 1978. Appendix: Minutes: Episcopal synod, May 6–10, 1978.

10. National Archives of Zimbabwe, file Ms.1036/10/6. Minutes: Anglican Church Mashonaland Diocesan standing committee, September 14, 1978.

Religious Leadership in National Political Conflicts

gave Africans at least a semblance of political power. But because it left the control of the nation—the armed forces, the police, the civil service, and the economy—effectively in the hands of the whites, Zimbabwe-Rhodesia did not win international recognition, although it looked for a time as if the new British Conservative Government of Margaret Thatcher might be pressured by its right wing into doing so. Moreover, Salisbury's main hope that the guerrillas could now be persuaded to surrender proved illusionary. To the nationalists at war this reconciliation appeared a sham, just as "Zimbabwe-Rhodesia" was a shameful name because it retained Cecil John Rhodes' name, implying continued white rule. The war intensified.

Mrs. Thatcher's Parliamentary private secretary Ian Gow is quoted as having told a story about Winston Churchill after World War II. Churchill was concerned about the political settlement in Greece and asked General Scobie, the British Commander in Athens, about Archbishop Damaskinos, the interim leader of the Greek government, "Are we dealing with a man of God, on his knees in daily supplication, or a scheming priest with political ambition?" Scobie answered, "I very much regret to say, Prime Minister, it's the latter." To which Churchill replied, "Then he's our man!"[11] Gow commented, "If there had been, at the head of the then internal Rhodesian government, a man of outstanding political skills and quality, a leader who commanded very considerable support within Rhodesia, then it might have been a different story." Gow expressed his regret: "One of the sadnesses about that period was that the Bishop, who I am sure was a man of God, was without any political skills at all."[12]

That was Ian Smith's own assessment in the end, although he still claimed that under the 1978 settlement when Muzorewa was Prime Minister he had relinquished control. DeWaal remarked, "They took poor old Bishop Muzorewa for a ride. He was not a politician; just a simple man of the Church and that was his rightful place. He didn't understand the game."[13] Defined as a "game," maybe the Bishop did not play the game. "Caring for the people in an orderly manner" might have been his political orientation. Maybe that is the result of the mix of church and state—a new game altogether.

Bishop Muzorewa was by now firmly locked into the Rhodesian government structure, not actually running anything but in a position where he had to take responsibility. For the nationalists the presence of Bishop Muzorewa as nominal head of state in the Zimbabwe-Rhodesia government

---

11. De Waal, *Politics of Reconciliation*, 32–33.
12. Edward, *Orientalism*, 33.
13. De Waal, *Politics of Reconciliation*, 33.

presented problems. Some rather naive outside observers began to ask what more the nationalists wanted now that there was a black man in office in Salisbury. Indeed as Bishop Muzorewa prepared to take office as Prime Minister, there were reports that the guerilla movements were losing the morale to fight. Some guerilla fighters were reported to be returning home to undergo rehabilitation and join the regime's army; others were reported to be seeking refuge in some African countries or Europe. But Nkomo and Mugabe told Dan Rather of CBS on April 22, 1978, that the war would go on until Zimbabwe was unconditionally free. Zimbabweans have always asked the question why Mugabe and Nkomo did not make the move to talk to Bishop Muzorewa and understand how they could take advantage of the concessions offered by Ian Smith to move toward total control. The two realized that doing so would have given Bishop Muzorewa an upper position in the final situation of total independence. Hence, at all costs Bishop Muzorewa had to be avoided. If anything, Mugabe and Nkomo would rather go on with the war, overrun the country, and establish a military rule. This was mainly Mugabe's objective—military rule as an instrument for permanent power. Till this day, Zimbabwe is run by a semi-military rule. If Bishop Muzorewa had seen this, what would he have done?

On April 28, 1978, the UN Security Council voted to reiterate its resolution of March 8 that the internal agreement was null and void. Britain and the United States abstained, suggesting that they wanted to keep their options open. As the war showed signs of escalation, both Bishop Muzorewa and Smith seemed to want to put the elections behind them and pay more attention to finding ways of ending the war.[14]

In this stance Bishop Muzorewa was fanning the fires of controversy at a time when he needed moderation in an effort to bridge the gap between him and other black political leaders. Now speaking the language Smith had been speaking for years, Bishop Muzorewa was making it harder for a peaceful solution to the problems of the country to be found.[15]

The internal settlement was not a permanent solution for Rhodesia's economic, social, and political problems. It proved to be fatal that the Patriotic Front had been left out of the Salisbury Agreement. Bishop Muzorewa and Rev. Sithole were not able to exert any political influence on the more militant nationalists on the basis of former ANC claims. Instead the armed liberation struggle escalated. Presumably Smith had hoped the Bishop would be able to stop the war. But all was in vain.

14. Ibid.
15. Ibid.

Religious Leadership in National Political Conflicts

In some areas guerillas were reported to be taking a more antagonistic stance toward local Christian congregations and institutions, as their perceived leaders were involved in the internal settlement.[16] However, in August 1978 there was a crisis in UANC when a distinct group of Protestant churchmen, including Revs. M. Chigwida, J. Kurewa and A. Kanodereka, strongly criticized the UANC leadership for signing the internal settlement agreement. They expressed sympathies with Byron Hove, who had earlier resigned from the UANC protesting the signing of the agreement. They were expelled from the party after the return of Bishop Muzorewa from another diplomatic mission in London. Prior to this, Garfield Todd had publicly denounced the internal settlement.[17]

The CCR found itself caught in the middle between moderate and militant nationalist approaches to the nation's problem. It did in fact qualify its position further in 1978 in such a way that it could take new and fresh political initiatives in favor of national unity and reconciliation toward independence. Garfield Todd's contribution was important in this process: with his positive relationship with Joshua Nkomo and his high appreciation for Robert Mugabe, he made a contribution in qualifying the stand of the CCR.[18] It sided less openly with the Muzorewa-led government and emphasized that a settlement was now required between nationalists inside the country and those fighting from outside. This would be another phase of disagreement among black leaders themselves, adding to the Victoria Falls, Lusaka, Geneva, and now Salisbury meetings.

The real pursuit of the ministry of reconciliation, which the CCR had anticipated in July 1978, was effectively initiated by the Council of Churches (whose name was changed to the Zimbabwe Council of Churches when the country became Zimbabwe-Rhodesia) when it held its annual general meeting on July 6, 1979. After reports of continued war and the suffering of displaced people in rural and urban Zimbabwe, the ZCC agreed on the following analysis and proposed plan of action: "As all Christians must work to do God's will in our society, we call first for recognition of the evils which confront us. We are a divided and suffering people. Hundreds of thousands of our children are without education, without adequate food and clothing."[19] The statement continued: "We appeal to all political leaders to

16. Hellencreutz, "Council in Cross Fire," 92.
17. *The Rhodesia Herald*, August 14, 1978.
18. Hellencreutz, *Religion and Politics*, 4.
19. ZCC executive committee, July 5, and annual meeting, July 6, 1979, note that the CCR changed its name to ZCC at the inception of Zimbabwe Rhodesia it deed not take

start immediate consultations to determine what must be done to restore peace to our land."[20]

To conclude, the statement declared, "We instruct our executive to make closer contact with our Churches throughout the world, providing them with information concerning the need of our people and of our land. We ask them for their prayers and for their moral and political support in our efforts to achieve peace for our country under the will of God."[21]

A theology of reconciliation was seen as the solution to the conflict. Negotiations were put in the forefront to resolve the conflict. War was condemned as a means of resolving the conflict because it was causing many people to not only suffer but die. Hence the ZCC could not simply watch; it had to make an ethical decision. Immediate contacts were made with the World Council of Churches (WCC), which had set aside part of its special fund for assistance to the war-displaced persons in Rhodesia.[22] At the same time, a special ZCC reconciliation committee was appointed to put into effect the major decision of the Council in the search for a lasting solution to the political crisis in the country.

This reconciliation committee decided to put its case directly before the Prime Minister of Zimbabwe-Rhodesia, Bishop Muzorewa, and the two leaders of the Patriotic Front, Robert Mugabe and Joshua Nkomo. The committee did meet Bishop Muzorewa in Salisbury but was not able to establish contacts with Mugabe in Maputo or Nkomo in Lusaka. Eventually British initiatives and the forthcoming Lancaster House Conference overtook the ZCC mission.[23] One wonders what might have come out of the ZCC initiative.

Bishop Muzorewa requested leave from his own church in June 1979 so that he could devote his time to attending to the demands of his new responsibility as Prime Minister. Retired Bishop Dodge was invited back as acting head of the denomination. Was this merely a matter of having too much work to handle the two roles, or did the Bishop feel uncomfortable about a possible incompatibility between the two roles? As soon as he became head of state, his church members had also been forced into a dual role, some joined his party, and others did not. Needless to say, this proved very difficult for many of them.

the Rhodesia part of the name of the country.
20. Ibid.
21. Ibid.
22. ZCC executive committee meeting, July 14, 1979.
23. Shiri, *My Visit*, 4.

Religious Leadership in National Political Conflicts

As Prime Minister of Zimbabwe-Rhodesia, the Bishop decided to go to the United States to seek American recognition for his government. So far only South Africa had recognized it, Great Britain had hesitated, and the United States was following the lead of the British, who still claimed responsibility for the former colony that had never been granted its independence. The Bishop hoped to see President Carter and other American politicians, including the right wing Senator Jesse Helms, who reportedly had sponsored his trip to the States.[24]

Still, as the Episcopal leader of The United Methodist Church in Rhodesia, he had informed the Secretary of the Council of Bishops of his visit to the United States. He was invited to meet with the leadership of the Council of Bishops. Bishop Roy Nichols of Pittsburgh, the President of the Council, asked Bishop Muzorewa if the Council could be helpful in any way during the Lancaster House talks, which were scheduled to begin in September. He suggested that perhaps some other Bishop might be temporarily assigned to supervise church affairs during Bishop Muzorewa's absence from Rhodesia. Bishop Dodge, who was present, noted, "It was merely a suggestion that he nodded to. We closed circle with arms on each other's shoulders and had a prayer for Bishop Muzorewa and his nation, still going through some turbulent times."[25]

The other Bishops tried to stand with Bishop Muzorewa as much as they could. They also tried to bring to his attention the fact that he needed someone to help pastor the church since he was full-time in politics. This moral and spiritual support shown by the leaders of The United Methodist Council of Bishops was an indication that Bishop Muzorewa was not breaking with the denomination's expectations of him as an Episcopal leader. Being involved politically in the national conflict with the hope of resolving it and bringing peace to the people of Zimbabwe was consistent with "making peace." However, while many colleagues supported Bishop Muzorewa, others were as apprehensive as the Christians in Zimbabwe-Rhodesia.

When Bishop Dodge arrived in the country he discovered that "the political situation was tragic in its divisiveness. Not only was the population divided, but also members of families were often separated from each other geographically, ideologically, and emotionally. . . . We [Bishop and Mrs. Dodge] felt these divisions and tried to remain politically neutral."[26]

24. Ibid., 188.
25. Ibid., 190.
26. Ibid., 192.

The interim bishop found his Episcopal work curbed by Bishop Muzorewa's political position. He noted, "I was eager to visit our rural churches but was warned against any such foolish attempt. Whether I desired it or not, I would be labeled pro-Muzorewa, just because we were both Methodist Bishops."[27] By this time much of rural Zimbabwe was dominated by Patriotic Front guerillas. The United Methodist Church was labeled "Muzorewa's Church," and in addition to that, there were not many churches that were still functional in the rural areas, given the Communist orientation of the Soviet and Chinese trained guerillas that dominated these areas. In spite of what people like Bishop Patrick Mutume (Catholic) were teaching about Jesus and God's love, villagers were terrorized by their sons and daughters (guerrillas) who came back from China, Tanzania, and Mozambique with Socialist or even Communist ideologies.

27. Ibid.

10

Lancaster House Agreement (1980)

THE LANCASTER HOUSE CONFERENCE was an all-parties constitutional conference held in London from September to December 1979 to resolve the Rhodesia crisis. It was at this conference that a final peace agreement was signed that led to the national elections that brought out majority rule in Zimbabwe. Most likely all parties involved were getting not only weary but bankrupt and hopeless.

Nkomo made a note that at Lancaster House it was hard for the Patriotic Front team to make personal contact with Bishop Muzorewa's team. Nkomo's opinion was that "the Bishop seemed to have decided that his only chance of political survival lay in sticking fast by the hard-line whites. He talked like an old-time settler, impatient with the talking, threatening to break off and go home, and saying: 'After all, I have a country to run.'"[1]

It is interesting to note the difference that had grown between the two men's positions over a period of just five years. Nkomo, who had dragged Bishop Muzorewa into politics, was now not comfortable with him. The Bishop was now talking about a country to run, not seeking peaceful agreement that would unite all Zimbabweans.

Ian Smith writes that at the Lancaster House talks people fooled the Bishop and gave him hope that he was going to be the Prime Minister after the elections. Smith noted: "The day had arrived for our government delegation to make their decision on the draft constitution. I felt genuine sorrow for Bishop Muzorewa because he was out of his depth, not really in the same league as the other players in the 'no-holds-barred' rough and tumble of international politics."

---

1. Nkomo, *Nkomo*, 201.

Lancaster House Agreement (1980)

Lord Carrington had almost assured the Bishop:

> Of course everyone knows that you are going to be the in-coming Prime Minister, so you may leave your slippers behind in your office to await your return. If Carrington had acted in keeping with the Lancaster House Agreement concerning parties which resort to intimidation during the election campaign, as will be recorded later, Muzorewa would have been Prime Minister, but for reasons of political expediency he changed his stance.[2]

In the light of such an assurance, one wonders why the Bishop trusted the Patriotic Front this time around.

As for the Zimbabwean churches' involvement in this process, a nucleus of four were entrusted to go to Lancaster House from ZCC and confer with all the Zimbabwean leaders. The four were Bishop Shiri, Revs. Siyachitema and Kuchera, and ZCC General Secretary Watyoka. The intention of this team was "to impress upon the three main actors on the Zimbabwean scene the need to end the war in Zimbabwe through political reconciliation."[3]

They managed to establish some rapport with the three different political delegations and were in fact recognized as a possible means of communication between them since, as noted from Nkomo's statement, earlier communication was proving difficult. They did not manage to arrange a joint meeting of the three delegations, and Bishop Shiri stated, "The reason was just the old British game of divide and conquer which the Chairman was playing skillfully."[4] It seems the British officials "organizing" this conference knew whom to allow to associate with whom.

Reconciliation and national unity were the primary concerns of the ZCC delegation to Lancaster House. Summarizing his report on the visit later, Bishop Shiri of the Lutheran Church stated, "I wish to point out the importance of unity. PF was successful at Lancaster House because they united. If UANC had joined hands with the other two parties as we suggested, the results would have been different."[5]

But Bishop Shiri did not know what Bishop Muzorewa had experienced with interacting with Nkomo and Mugabe. Chambati notes,

---

2. Ibid.
3. Garfield, *The Rhodesia Herald*, September 13, 1979.
4. Shiri, *My Visit*, 7.
5. Ibid., 10. A draft report had been presented to the ZCC Executive Committee at its meeting on January 22, 1980. The final version was tabled and approved but the executive on March 18, 1980. Cf. ZCC ex. com., January 22 and March 18.

Religious Leadership in National Political Conflicts

> On his return from the Lancaster House Conference, the Bishop was confident that he had the support of a large section of the African population, enough to earn him victory at the elections in 1980. He disregarded the fact that the UANC had become an enemy of the black people. It was impossible for the Africans to forget what the Bishop had done during the time of the internal rule.[6]

This feeling was clearly demonstrated at the time of elections in March 1980, when the UANC won only three seats out of one hundred in the Zimbabwean Parliament despite vigorous campaigns using helicopters and small aircraft. They probably spent more money on the campaign than the two wings of the PF put together.

Bishop Ralph Dodge, who was still acting as head of The United Methodist Church in Zimbabwe when Bishop Muzorewa was running in the election, convened a seminar for his people on Reconciliation, Reconstruction and Religious Revival in the Tribal Trust Lands.[7] This was in an effort to heal wounds and prepare the church for reconciliation. The Bishop was being more focused and expecting the end of the conflict. Everyone in his church anxiously awaited the results of the February elections. Bishop Dodge wrote, "We gathered around the tea table at the office to hear the results over the radio: UANC3; ZAPU-PF20; ZANU-PF57. There was no question about who would be the next Prime Minister."[8]

Bishop Dodge congratulated the new Prime Minister: "I wrote Mr. Robert Mugabe a letter congratulating him and his party; I wrote a note of condolence to Bishop Muzorewa, whose party had lost badly even though the Bishop himself had won a seat in Parliament."[9]

Bishop Dodge had hoped that Bishop Muzorewa might now resign from politics and give himself exclusively to church work. He had served his country well and should now let others carry the burden. This could have been the thinking of many more people in the church so that the efforts of the reconciliation program initiated by Bishop Dodge would bear fruits. But Bishop Muzorewa did accept the results of the election and prepared to leave the office of head of state. Although Bishop Muzorewa did not give up the leadership of the UANC, he asked for a few more months to rest after the campaign. Dodge wrote, "Bishop Muzorewa asked that we [Bishop and Mrs.

6. Chambati, "National Unity-ANC," 158.
7. Hellencreutz, *Religion and Politics*, 450.
8. Dodge, *Revolutionary Bishop*, 194.
9. Ibid.

Dodge] remain for another three months, to give him time to turn the keys of government over to Mr. Mugabe, and then have a period of rest. At Bishop Muzorewa's request, the Council of Bishops extended our assignment for another three months."[10]

Finally the independence celebration of Zimbabwe was set for April 18, 1980. Bishop Muzorewa was a Member of Parliament until 1985 and then continued to head the UANC as its president. He made further efforts to win the national presidency in 1996 and finally resigned altogether from politics in 2000.

---

10. Ibid., 198.

11

Reflections of People Who Were Involved with Bishop Muzorewa

CHART 1

Question: Based on the experience of 1970s, how can religious leaders assist in processing effective reconciliation in an open national conflict?

Group Name	Responses
Liberation war nationalists	-Religious leaders use influence, they do not use command. People respect religious leaders because of their positions in society; they earn their respect. -I expect religious leaders to continue rebuking errant rulers. My philosophy is that what the Bible teaches is what we would call the secular laws of the country. The teaching of the Bible has become the common law of any country. -These days religious leaders are being intimidated, but the church must always be involved to give influence from its point of view. Every ruler stops to listen when the Pope speaks because they seek an opportunity to get a blessing from the Pope. -When there is lots of controversy, look for a religious figure, draw him to the centre *munombotonhora* ("you will be stilled"). We liked clergy because they had a platform, and they could speak from their pulpits. They were real people of courage, so we naturally liked them. -Religious leaders have a stature that attracts people from all corners. They have a uniting influence, an image that is inherent in a religious leader. They have an all-around acceptability. The nationalists appreciated the religious leaders since the centre of every human being is religious.

Reflections of People Who Were Involved with Bishop Muzorewa

United Methodist Church Members	-Religious leaders should stand as mediators, reconcilers, and peacemakers, and not take a political line in terms of party politics. -Desmond Tutu is a good example of what a bishop should do.
United Methodist Church members in the UANC leadership	-As religious leaders we need to understand what is going on in our world and help our congregations to understand the political views. Our people are being cheated during elections because they do not have information. As religious leaders we should be in a position where we can influence political leaders. -I think we have the capacity to influence events as religious leaders. We need not look at all politicians as bad people; some may be corrupt, but some are there because that is where they should be. Their participation in politics is a calling. We should recognize them so that we can influence them; they are not always moving away from God.
Bishop Muzorewa	-It is the duty of Christian leaders to go to political leaders to rebuke, as Nathan the prophet did. Have courage to rebuke take the risk of what political leaders may do to you. Every person basically is a coward, but what makes a person courageous or even dangerously courageous is the conviction of the vocation. -Jesus speaks of the liberation of people in Luke 4:18–19. -We should be a source of encouragement to people, to reconcile the people. -If you are convinced that you have the Word of God, you are the voice of God in the situation. -Be honest and frank; there is no limit to what you can say. Never take sides with any of the parties in conflict. -Point the nation in the right direction, toward political prosperity and salvation, leading to the economic prosperity of the country.

Religious Leadership in National Political Conflicts

Other current religious leaders	-There is no one common way to do it. We need many people who do not fear and are convinced that what they are doing is what God wants them to do. Speak your mind truthfully without insulting anyone. The church will have a voice in a conflict situation. If you say there is corruption, be loud and clear in what you say. People should believe that God is calling them. Pastors must take this form of ministry as a vocation. -If you read Luke 4, then we have a mandate to serve the people. -Religious leaders should always stand on the truth. We should maintain a degree of neutrality when it comes to party politics. We can take the example of Archbishop Desmond Tutu of South Africa—he stood firmly against apartheid, proclaimed the message of democracy, justice, rule of law, and respect for human rights. He maintained a position as a prophet giving a prophetic message to the nation, urging South Africans to fight for their rights. -It is our responsibility as the church to help in a situation that looks bad and threatening to human life and dignity. Religious leaders have a role to help a conflict situation develop into a peaceful situation and achieve human dignity and recognition of basic human rights. There is no apology to make when we demand respect for human dignity; it is part of our vocation. If we preach the message of loving one another and loving one's neighbor, we can actually go further and do what Jesus did; we can even define who the neighbor is. And that is part of our public ministry.

SUMMARY COMMENTS

All the groups reflected that influence is the best approach religious leaders can use to assist in an open national conflict. Neutrality was also seen as an important stance that religious leaders need to maintain as they are faced with a conflict if they are to help resolve it.

Courage is expected of religious leaders, and this is born of a sense that their work is a vocation and a responsibility.

It is interesting to note that only the rank and file membership of the church stressed the importance of a leader's primary role as reconciliatory, while other pointed more to the need for the religious leader to denounce the wrong.

Reflections of People Who Were Involved with Bishop Muzorewa

The words of Jesus Christ in the Gospel of St. Luke mentioned by two respondents are enough of a mandate to be involved if there is a conflict based on injustice. The passage referred to reads, "The spirit of the Lord is upon me, because he has anointed me to preach the gospel to the poor; he has sent me to heal the brokenhearted, to proclaim liberty to the captives and recovery of sight to the blind, to set at liberty those who are oppressed; to proclaim the acceptable year of the Lord" (Luke 4:18–19).

The national liberation fighters' comments show an interesting reflection on the convergence between Christian spirituality and political ideology at the point of human ontology. Two respondents who were veterans of the armed struggle for independence emphasized the point that "religious leaders should stand as mediators, reconcilers, and peacemakers, and not take a political line." It should be remembered that the guerillas were always opposed to Bishop Muzorewa's leadership, creating a serious difference of opinion on this point with their national party leaders in ZANU and ZAPU.

CHART 2

Question: Are there any limitations on the role of the religious leaders in an open national political conflict?

Group Names	Responses
Liberation war nationalists	-No limitations. Perhaps avoid being deeply involved in the controversy of political divisions; but there are situations where they should stand and continue to be counted. -If there is tribalism such as in the Rwandan case, they should have stood up against it rather than being in the centre of it.
The United Methodist Church Members	-Bishop Muzorewa went too far by leading a political party. -The example of Bishop Muzorewa is a good one, but only up to the Pearce Commission; he should not have gone further. -When church leaders decide to be in politics, they should not bring it into the church. We come to church to worship God, not to do political business. Religious leaders who get involved in party politics should take time to explain to people that their political parties have nothing to do with the church.

United Methodist Church members in the UANC leadership	-Bishop Dodge had a way to influence political leaders. He was not directly involved in politics, but there is no politician of his time who did not go to his office to share their views. Nationalists such as Nkomo, Sithole, Chitepo, and many others went to spend time with Bishop Dodge, sharing their views and seeking his advice.
Bishop Muzorewa	-Dr Kenneth Kaunda said politics is dangerous, threatening, but someone's child has to do it. So there should be no limitation. Do as God send you.
Other current religious leaders	-It is important to know that the political party is the most difficult thing to change. So it is not wise for religious leaders to be partisan because it will be difficult to leave once you are there. Stand in a position were politicians come to share their views. -As long as humans are sinners, there is no limitation. -As long as there are suffering people, we (church leaders) cannot afford to sit back and watch, expecting that the politicians will do something about it.

SUMMARY COMMENTS

Responses ranged from "There are no limitations" to putting a ban on overt association with a political party in competition with other parties. The comment that "political parties have nothing to do with the church" speaks loudly. Evidently it is the specific situation that dictates the way to go for most respondents. The religious leaders speak on the basis of addressing the ills of society until the end. It is interesting to note the sentiment expressed by one United Methodist Church member who felt that the political affiliation of the Bishop had penetrated his message and role in the church, which was unacceptable.

CHART 3

Question: How did the Bishop consult you for advice in his role as a political figure? What did you advise him?

Group Name	Responses
Liberation war nationalists	-I do not know much about that, but I think he consulted his clergy members -I was not in the ANC Council, so I had no opportunity to work with him.
United Methodist Church members	-He consulted people around the country. Some said he should drop from politics, saying the ethical issues arising from a church leader being in a political party were not clear. Unity had been achieved, but now his party was becoming the opposition. -We did not meet with him to consult; we could only meet him at revivals or at political rallies.
United Methodist Church members in the UANC leadership	-As we interacted with the bishop, he consulted us. In that interaction he influenced lots of youth to go to war as freedom fighters. I was certain that he was doing a good thing. At every United Methodist Church annual conference, the Church and Society Committee would give him the mandate to continue in pursuit of the liberation of the people of Zimbabwe. -We would tell him of our support of his actions. -In 1978 during the internal settlement negotiations, no one could come out openly because external parties were changing their approach. Some members began to leave and raise other voices. By 1979, we were facing changes. -My view is that the bishop had many consultants known only to him. -His decision to be involved in the ANC movement has roots elsewhere; he did not consult us, but many of us supported him. In the movement to block the Pearce Commission, many churches supported him. -During the UANC period, I would say he would consult with us. The bishop used to come to our place to discuss. We would encourage him to move on. But during the internal settlement negotiations, we advised him to stop and consult with the outside liberation movements. These people formed the ANC when they were in prison, and they were the ones who had invited him into politics.

Bishop Muzorewa	-Before I accepted the invitation to lead the ANC, I consulted the Annual Conference (of my Church) at Old Mutare in 1972. The Annual Conference unanimously voted to let me be involved; there was even a vote carried out at the annual conference. Thereafter I was consulting individual church members. -Consultation of people is my practice in the church. I would consult conference lay leaders and district superintendents when I wanted to make a decision, as well as other lay groups and individuals.

SUMMARY COMMENTS

The question of how the bishop consulted his main constituents both in the church and in the political field is important to this research because it relates directly to the way he interpreted his mandate within the situation. It is evident from the above that the church members officially connected to the UANC constitute the only group that is confident that there was adequate consultation by the bishop. Another issue raised by the responses is the bishop's choice between the different voices he was hearing as the consultation seems to have evoked conflicting responses. From the expectations of his main constituents in both the church members and the nationalists, the bishop had to sieve their voices through his own reading of demands on his leadership.

CHART 4

Question: What were Bishop Muzorewa's political, spiritual, and doctrinal expectations in participating in the political process?

Group Names	Responses
Liberation war nationalists	-We wanted him to champion the cause of the struggle to oppose the constitutional proposals that the British were planning as a means for granting independence to Rhodesia. -He had no terms, but he did a good job. Nationalists like Zvobgo and Edson Sithole (ZANU) and others from ZAPU were supporting him. -The Smith-Home constitutional proposals were dangerous. If the British had granted Rhodesia independence, then the liberation of Zimbabwe was going to be difficult. Bishop Muzorewa was asked to save the situation at that crucial moment.
United Methodist Church members in the UANC leadership	-In terms of religious values in politics, we need to know that you may not win an election simply because you are a Christian. You need other principles. What becomes more important are the political views. -He stood as a Bishop in his faith. The UANC manifesto had Christian values. He continued to cherish the guerilla's work. -He tried to fight for peace. -Acceptance of the election results in 1980 was a Christian value. We may have had no peace if he had not been a Christian and accepted defeat at the polls.
Bishop Muzorewa	-When you love people, as leader you decide with the people at heart. I love people, and liberation decisions must be made in the context of love. I listened through prayer and meditation, guided by the social principles of our church, which teach freedom.

SUMMARY COMMENTS

The bishop fulfilled the politicians' expectations in terms of saving a situation that was politically tricky. All the groups agreed that the bishop brought Christian values to the situation. The bishop himself says he was motivated by his love for the people; he wanted the people to be free. The acceptance of the election results by the Bishop in 1980 and the handover of power to a new government is highly valued.

Concerning the relationship between religious and political roles, all the groups were asked to examine the case study and comment on the conflict between the roles that the Bishop played.

CHART 5

Question: Did the two roles (church and politics) compromise or hinder each other's effectiveness in any way?

Group Number	Responses
Liberation war nationalists	-No religious limitations were required of his political role; if he had any they were not so much because of religion but because of personal choices. -There was no compromise; he did a good job. -At Lusaka the Bishop should not have accepted the cease-fire proposals. Maybe his Christian principles motivated him to accept cease-fire. He should have given us the go-ahead to fight. He should have left the war front to us, and he would have come home to lead the political home front.
United Methodist Church members	-There was confusion; there were times when we were embarrassed to be known as members of The United Methodist Church because of the party political image that this portrayed. -There were days when the Bishop would go missing from the pulpit or other church activities. The involvement of the Bishop divided the church. Many church members even became enemies. They are still clashing today based on their divisions during the experiences of the 1970s. -It is an experience we wish had never happened. -It was a trying time. We lost a number of our members during that period. I only thank God that some of the members went to other denominations. At least the Christian church did not completely lose them.

Reflections of People Who Were Involved with Bishop Muzorewa

The United Methodist Church members in the UANC leadership	-There was some compromise of the office of the Bishop. The war was going on, and there were some killings. It was difficult for the Bishop to stand independent of the issues. The bishop's office was compromised. -The army would go on a rampage. As head of state and Commander in Chief of the army, the bishop would have to support them. At a military level the bishop was compromised. The public could not separate the church from the UANC.
Bishop Muzorewa	-I saw them complementing each other. During my time as political leader, my Christian principles made me abstain from unchristian politics. I went with the principle that politics has no place in Christianity, but Christianity has a place in politics. My Christian leadership would Christianize politics, although politics would have no place in the church. -However there is an element of ineffectiveness when you do not go along with the hardliner, ruthless nationalist. You think about forgiveness while they think of violence and the physical elimination of opponents. When guided by a Christian spirit, it becomes a political weakness.

SUMMARY COMMENTS

Generally the responses show that the Bishop's Episcopal role was overshadowed by his political role. His contemporary religious leaders were asked the same question but were not as comfortable in making a comparison of the two roles that Bishop Muzorewa played. The general church membership felt that the bishop's political involvement divided the church and the effects became long lasting. This is not surprising given that the church membership is made up of citizens who have various political alignments. If an Episcopal leader leading a specific political party allows his political leaning to prejudice his relationship with members of other persuasions, there is a problem. Some respondents felt this had happened. Even some of the former UANC leaders felt the religious office had been sacrificed and some moral religious values were also sacrificed when they spoke of the Bishop's military leadership as head of state. This in part answers the third question of the study about how far into the political arena a religious leader can go and still

Religious Leadership in National Political Conflicts

be helpful in resolving a national conflict while remaining true to his or her primary calling in the church.

A look at other resources beyond the interviews is helpful here. Bishop Muzorewa noted that throughout the period of his political activity he continued his responsibilities as United Methodist Church bishop. He wrote in his autobiography that sometimes the two roles collided with embarrassing results not only for him but also for others.[1] It is important for religious leaders to realize that as they try to resolve national political conflicts, working within a shifting political system, for whatever reason, can compromise one's values. It can whet one's appetite for power, blunt one's judgment, and finally expose one's human side of powerlessness by cooption into the system. The situation calls for extreme vigilance.

Bishop Muzorewa has told movingly how he wrestled in prayer to reach his decision to surrender the premiership to further the cause of peace at the Lancaster House Conference.[2] From the beginning, when Ian Smith declared his Rhodesia Front to be ushering "Christian civilization" into the country, the church was brought into the political arena. It had to stand and challenge the moral ways of racism and human rights abuse. This must be understood as the background that nurtured Bishop Muzorewa's public engagement. The fact that he was the only black Zimbabwean head of a denomination at that time put him into the spotlight immediately and gave him special responsibility.

Evidently, the Bishop began his political career reluctantly. Edgar Tekere, the veteran nationalist politician, said:

> Bishop Muzorewa was well postured in the church. We all admired his braveness to speak against the ills of the Rhodesia Government. When we smuggled our invitation letter to Muzorewa to take up leadership of the ANC, he refused to lead the ANC. We tried three times, and he simply said, "Please, I am a church man, leave me out of politics." Finally he accepted. That is when we asked all ZANU supporters to rally behind the Bishop as the leader. Later we in ZANU realized that while we were persuading Bishop Muzorewa to lead the "No" vote (in the Pearce Commission referendum), those in ZAPU who were in prison in Gonakudzingwa were also persuading him to lead the "No" vote on their behalf. That is how Bishop Muzorewa came to lead the ANC.

---

1. Muzorewa, *Rise Up and Walk*, 135.
2. De Wall, *Politics of Reconciliation*, 34.

Reflections of People Who Were Involved with Bishop Muzorewa

Tekere's testimony is important because it indicates Bishop Muzorewa's original stance. Evidently he saw an unsolvable contradiction between political and religious leadership at the time. Bishop Muzorewa says that in 1974 he offered to resign from the political leadership of the ANC since the detainees were now out of detention and they were able to choose a person who would lead the ANC. He says, "I walked out so that they would do their business. When they called me back they told me that they had unanimously agreed that I should lead them. That is when the United ANC was formed, but unfortunately the unity did not last long. Divisions emerged; power rather than purpose started pulling people apart."

While the Bishop responded to the public demands of the political situation, there were also the demands of his church members, both as a specially identified responsibility and as a cross section of society. Here the Bishop was faced with two groups of people who were sometimes in fierce discord. The Bishop confirmed that there were some in The United Methodist Church who advised him to leave party politics He noted that at one time,

> A friend came to say, "If you are really a bishop, you should quit politics and the ANC." I knew that he represented a considerable number of clergy and laity of our church, both black and white, who were against my involvement in politics. They felt that I was out of step by being both Bishop of The United Methodist Church and leader of the ANC in Zimbabwe. Shortly thereafter a relative who usually did not comment about my work also came and said, "I want to propose that you quit ANC. Please listen to me."

On another occasion the Bishop was approached by a young woman church member who said to him,

> Please, please, my Bishop, you should now cease to be president of the ANC and stick to the church. What you have done so far is enough. Your life is now very short. You are going to be murdered very soon. Also some people, even those in high places in the church, are criticizing you for being in the ANC. They are saying, "We do not have a bishop." Please listen to me although I am younger and of a lower office in the Church than you are.[3]

The bishop's reaction to that occasion shows mixed feelings

> I listened carefully. Looking at Maggie [Mrs. Muzorewa], I felt she was looking at the young lady as if to say, "Tell him; perhaps he will listen to you because I have often told him the same thing." I

---

3. Muzorewa, *Rise Up and Walk*, 147.

thanked the young lady for coming to register her loving concern. But as she spoke I remembered the words of Jesus, "Get thee behind me, Satan"—words the Master addressed to Peter when he wanted Jesus to avoid a confrontation with his enemies.[4]

In the research interview he added, "By accepting the principal of liberation it means you have to be involved. It also means leadership. Dr. Kenneth Kaunda once said, 'Politics is dangerous, threatening, and nasty, but someone's child has to do it.'"[5]

While Church leaders consult people in their decision making, there are also demands that arise from a highly subjective ethical response to one's calling, usually informed by church doctrine and historical precedent. Bishop Muzorewa noted that when he prayed, God told him that the liberation of people was God's business, and that motivated the bishop to take up political leadership. "That was the main voice in me throughout in the decision-making process," the bishop goes on to say. At the moment he was involved in the politics of Zimbabwe, the major pushing factor was love of the people. "There were other voices to the back of my mind, like that of Martin Luther King. I had attended one of his rallies in the USA. Also the teachings of Mahatma Gandhi on nonviolence. These were my leading principles."[6]

Speaking on the prompting of one's personal vocation, Bishop Bakare noted, "When God calls you, no matter where you are, whatever you are, God will use you as his instrument to achieve his mission." For some people Bishop Muzorewa was doing what people never expected him to do. But Bishop Sebastin Bakare says, "You can never tell when or how God can make use of you." It has been persuasively argued that the significance of the war for the churches lay not at the level of institutional pronouncements upon it but at the level of participation of churchmen in the sufferings of local rural communities.

Concerning the voices that articulated a calling of the religious leader into the political arena, Bishop Bakare responded in the interview: "Prophets of the eighth century like Amos were sent with a message of justice. Therefore every religious leader should ask the question, 'What is God calling me to do?' The issues of justice are a voice on their own; when there is no justice, there is no preaching of the Good News. Religious leaders get involved in politics as they make an effort to see to it that justice is practiced."

---

4. Ibid., 155.
5. Ibid.
6. Interview with Bishop Muzorewa, Harare, April 28, 2005.

Reflections of People Who Were Involved with Bishop Muzorewa

"I never thought I would be in political leadership," said Bishop Muzorewa. "But I have always believed that it is my duty to talk justice and advocate for justice. I made pronouncements against the Smith regime's oppressive systems in search for justice for the people of Zimbabwe." Several church members and nationalist leaders as well as the other religious leaders agree that Bishop Muzorewa was called by God to save the nation at a crucial time. However, as evidenced from the interviews, most respondents would confine this "crucial time" to the period of the Pearce Commission debate, whereas Bishop Muzorewa himself saw his role throughout the 1970s as an inevitable response of faith to a crucial time.

Listing four groups who gave him the mandate, Bishop Muzorewa said,

> My first mandate was from God. When I prayed about it I had the answer saying, "Go for it!" The liberation of people is my business. Second, the annual conference at Old Mutare gave me the mandate to be involved at public leadership level. The third mandate came from the political leaders who were in detention. All of them gave me the mandate to lead the political movement. Then finally the nationalist national leaders who were members of the deferent political parties.

The Bishop indicated that he did not continue seeking the mandate of his Church as he was getting involved at deferent levels, that is to say, when the ANC became a political party and when he became president of the UANC and later Prime Minister. He did not continue to seek the voice of the church, assuming it had already been given to him.

The debate within the church, which might have influenced his decision-making more directly had it been encouraged, would have picked up on the Bishop's statement above. Was there any possible alternative of the Bishop's leading of the UANC and the Zimbabwe-Rhodesia Government as he sought to fulfill the commandment of God's liberation business? Secondly, did the mandate given to the Bishop in December 1972 by the members of The United Methodist Church annual conference to "get involved" go so far as creating his own political party and taking it to the national elections in 1980? Thirdly, when the nationalist leaders withdrew their support from his leadership, was the Bishop aware that continued involvement on his own platform was no longer a fulfillment of the nationalist party wishes? His statement raises very clearly the importance of his personal interpretation of God's call, the church members consent, and the nationalist politicians' wishes.

Religious Leadership in National Political Conflicts

A former member of the Ian Smith's Rhodesian Front Army responded to the interview by narrating some events that demonstrate the values the Bishop brought into politics. "If the Bishop had had no Christian values, there would have been no peace in Zimbabwe. When he went to negotiate for the constitution at Lancaster House, he wanted all political parties to be involved. Those who were in the UANC and in the Zimbabwe-Rhodesia Government said that when the negotiations were going on in London, Smith cabled home that Prime Minister Muzorewa was betraying them. He tried to work a vote of no confidence on the prime minister, and then General Peter Walls, who was the Rhodesian Front's Military commander, would stage a military takeover. Walls refused and declared his allegiance to the Bishop." Here at least is one voice that sees the Bishop's leadership all the way to 1980 as essential to the conclusion of a peace agreement.

12

Conclusion

IN THIS BOOK I establish the understanding that it is the church's duty to offer constructive criticism to government on a wide range of issues. There must be separation of church and state for this to take place. Just as a free judiciary will promote the rule of law, so a free church will promote the rule of ethical principles and of morality. The church will need to continue to fight for justice. It is gravely regrettable that there are in Africa many instances where the church has remained silent in the face of injustice, oppression, and evil, in the face of nepotism, corruption, and oppression of one group of people against another. The church needs modern-day Nathans, the prophet of the Old Testament who did not hesitate to tell King David where he had gone wrong.

In this research, I have seen that Zimbabwe's political leaders in the run-up to 1980 did not generally see a contradiction between their political principles and Christian principles. Rather, they believed them to be basically in harmony. They explicitly appealed for the church's cooperation in their political agenda. The response to these overtures from the church was cautious. Zimbabwe's churches, having learned from this period in history, continue to make their voices heard in public statements and personal influence, but their stance is one of "critical solidarity" rather than affiliation with the state. This can be uncomfortable for any government, for while the state may be grateful for the solidarity, it may well also resent the criticism.

I have discovered that under the Smith regime the Roman Catholic bishops became increasingly identified with the liberation movement while the leaders of the Protestant churches, believing that they could influence government policy best behind the scenes, became tolerant of an internal settlement with Ian Smith. Each conflict that tears a nation apart will be met by extreme differences in the leanings of the church as a whole, and individual religious leaders will have to make their decisions within this polemic. Politicians recognize a difference of opinion between the churches and can take advantage of the disunity. At independence in Zimbabwe the party that won the elections, ZANU (PF), found the Catholic Church historically aligned in its favor and took advantage of this in the new dispensation.

It is important always to remember that the church responds to spiritual guidance, which is beyond the reach of politics. In The United Methodist Church in the war leading up to national independence in 1980, there was a boldness of conviction that went beyond fear of political recrimination. Christians continued to meet in their homes secretly to pray for their children who were fighting among the guerillas and for independence, even after their religious meetings had been banned by the liberation armies and their church buildings had been destroyed. Evidently their loyalty to the nationalist cause was not in opposition to their Christian ethics. When the Lancaster House Conference was convened in London on September 10, 1979, one could have said the resultant Zimbabwean independence was not due to the work of politicians and the liberation movements alone; the church was also involved. The church fed, clothed, and gave shelter to the freedom fighters, and it prayed for genuine settlement and political independence to come to a new Zimbabwe.

Another major lesson we have learned is that it is dangerous for religious leaders to be involved in party politics, but it is the duty of the religious leaders to lead the church to be the conscience of political players and governments. Religious leaders need to maintain their prophetic role in situations of conflict, to stand for what is right and good for the people. The issues of justice are indeed God's business; the servants of God are called to be his instruments to speak against injustice, abuse of human rights, and violations of human dignity. In doing this religious leaders need to be careful not to be carried by political agendas and power politics—they too take up issues of justice. The preference of the church should always be to keep a critical distance from government, keeping in mind Martin Luther King's Jr.'s statement that the church must not be the master or servant or instrument of the state but the conscience of the state. Religious leadership in every era must make its own decisions based on the situation of the time, the basic ethical questions that arise, and the guidance of fellow believers.

To conclude, it is important to note that although Bishop Muzorewa suffered a crushing defeat in the elections of 1980, this man of God gave himself for the freedom of Zimbabwe. Throughout the war he struggled daily with his conscience, tortured by the need to balance the people's expectations of him and his understanding of God's expectations in his life. He saw the people's need for freedom and dignity and recognized the possibility that he was well placed to assist them to attain these. I personally pay tribute to Bishop Abel Tendekayi Muzorewa for relentlessly working toward attainment of the goals and objectives that had for many years been the dream of Zimbabweans. He made outstanding personal sacrifices in order to do this. It was unfortunate that the signing of the internal agreement with Ian Smith was a moment judged by history as a moment of his poor judgment. But with the advent of Zimbabwe, Bishop Muzorewa could not be regarded as a loser because he helped that event to come about as no other person could. He accepted defeat in the 1980 elections with grace and dignity, recognizing, as very few African leaders have done, that the wishes of the voters must be respected. It is a lesson that all people must learn.

Epilogue

First it is recommended that further research be undertaken to understand the extent and limits of public expectations of religious leaders in solving political problems and offering leadership in the public arena. More could be learned from the examples of other religious leaders in Zimbabwe's history. People like Garfield Todd, Ndabaningi Sithole, Canaan Banana, Pius Ncube, Patrick Mutume, Sebastin Bakare, and Obadiah Musindo have actively participated in national politics.

Second, research is needed into the reconciliation policy pronounced by the Zimbabwe Government at independence in 1980 to investigate the extent to which it covered all the factions in the political society and where it fell short of embracing the nation as a whole. This would be based on the assumption by the churches prior to independence that they could influence the future unity of the country by appealing to nationalist politicians for what was revealed in this study.

Third, I recommend to the institutions training clergy in Africa and the world over that they collaborate to hold a pan-African workshop on religious leadership in situations of national crisis. The purpose would be to help religious leaders reflect on the conflict situations in Africa and see how to interpret their mandates in the face of public pressure and national need. This study would contribute to their debate on how far a religious leader can go without compromising his or her primary calling in the church

Lastly, I recommend that the schools of theology in Africa introduce courses on conflict management and conflict resolution, civil society, and governance. This will be an essential aspect of capacity building in the church, preparing future religious leaders who are likely to face open national political conflict. Zimbabwe with the rest of Africa is crying for contemporaries in the likes of Bishop Abel Tendekayi Muzorewa, Archbishop Desmond Tutu, Rev. Canaan Banana, Rev. Ndabaningi Sithole, Rev. Allen Boesak, Bishop Sabastin Bakare, Bishop Patrick Mutume, and Garfield Toddy, to mention but a few who were called to their nations at critical moments to champion peace, justice, human rights, democracy, and good governance.

Appendix

Interview Questionnaires

Group One: The Liberation War Movements' Nationalists

1. Why did the politicians look at religious leadership in the political conflict during the years under review (1970s)?
2. What did the politicians expect from Bishop Muzorewa in the political arena?
3. What limitations did Bishop Muzorewa have because of his religious background?
4. What terms were spelled out when he was invited to lead the ANC?
5. How and who did the Bishop consult for advice on his role in the political field, and what was he hearing?
6. Based on that experience of 1975–80, what is the most effective way that religious leaders can assist in an open national conflict?
7. What limitations should there be on the role of the religious leaders in an open national political conflict?

Group Two: The United Methodist Church Members

1. How did the Bishop consult you and other members on his political involvement?
2. What did you say to him?

Appendix

3. In your opinion, did the two roles compromise or hinder each other (making the one less effective) in any way?
4. Based on the United Methodist Church experience of 1975–80, what is the most effective way that religious leaders can assist in an open national political conflict?
5. Based on the United Methodist Church's experiences, what limitations should there be on the role of religious leaders in the political arena?

Group Three: United Methodist Church Members in the UANC Leadership

1. As a church member in political struggle, how did the Bishop in his role in the political arena consult you? What did you tell him?
2. In your own opinion, did the roles compromise or hinder each other in any way?
3. What values do you think the Bishop was able to bring from religious leadership to political leadership?
4. Based on your experience in 1975–80, what is the most effective way that religious leaders can assist in an open national political conflict? What limitations should there be on the role of the religious leader?

Group Four: Bishop Muzorewa

1. What motivated your involvement in the political conflict of Zimbabwe? What voice were you listening to and how?
2. How did you consult church members and political leaders as you made your political decisions?
3. How did you listen to your own spiritual understanding based on Christian ethics, the church's social principles, and Christian leadership?
4. How did you interpret the discipline of the United Methodist Church and your political involvement?

Appendix

5. What other voices influenced you or gave you advice about the political role that you were playing?
6. Did your two roles compromise of hinder each other (making the one less effective) in any way?
7. On the basis of your experience in life, what is the most effective way that religious leaders can assist in an open national political conflict? What limitations should there be on the role of the religious leader?

Group Five: Current Religious Leaders

1. How did you define your role during 1975–80 in response to the national political conflict?
2. What voices influenced you other than inner voices, and how did you interpret your obligation as church leaders in the political arena and in ministry?
3. In listening to those voices, how did you settle for voices that clash?
4. What is your comment on Bishop Muzorewa's involvement? Do you feel that his two roles compromise or hinder each other in a way? Can you give examples?
5. Based on that experience of 1975–80, what is the most effective way that religious leaders can assist in an open national political conflict?
6. What limitations should there be on the role of religious leaders?
7. What other views would you like to share on the topic?

Bibliography

Banana, C. S. 1982. *Theology of Promise: The Dynamics of Self Reliance*. Harare: College Press.
———, ed. 1989. *Turmoil and Tenacity: Zimbabwe 1890–1990*. Harare: College Press.
———. 1996. *The Church in the Struggle for Zimbabwe*. Gweru: Mambo.
Bennett, J. C. 1956. *The Christian as Citizen*. London: Lutherworth.
Bonhoeffer, D. 1956. *The Cost of Discipleship*. New York: Macmillan.
———. 1960. *Ethics*. London: SCM.
———. 1965. *No Rusty Swords*. New York: Harper and Row.
———. 1966. *Letters and Papers from Prison*. New York: Macmillan.
———. 1977. *Prayers from Prison*. Philadelphia: Fortress.
Brooks, E. H. 1960. *The City of God and the Politics of Crisis*. London: Oxford University Press.
Brown, R. McAfee. 1986. *Saying Yes and Saying No on Rendering to God and Caesar*. Philadelphia: Westminister.
Carson, H. M. 1957. *The Christian and the State*. London: Tyndale.
Chambati, A. M. 1989. "National Unity-ANC," in *Turmoil and Tenacity*, edited by C. S. Banana, 147–61.
De Waal, V. 1990. *The Politics of Reconciliation: Zimbabwe's First Decade*. London: Hurst.
DeWolf, L. H. 1971. *Responsible Freedom*. New York: Harper and Row.
Dodge, R. E. 1964. *The Unpopular Missionary*. Westwood, NJ: Fleming H. Revell.
———. 1986. *The Revolutionary Bishop Who Saw God at Work in Africa: Bishop Ralph E. Dodge: An Autobiography*. Pasadena: William Carey Library.
Edward, W. 1985. *Orientalism*. London: Penguin.
Eidsmoe, J. 1984. *God and Caesar: Christian Faith and Political Action*. Westchester: Crossway.
Fanon, F. 1986. *Black Skin and White Masks*. London: Pluto.
Gutiérrez, G. 1974. *A Theology of Liberation*. London: SCM.
Hallencreutz, C. F., and A. Moyo, eds. 1988. *Church and State in Zimbabwe*. Gweru: Mambo.
Hallencreutz, C. F. 1988. "A Council in Crossfire: ZCC 1964–1980," in *Church and State in Zimbabwe*, edited by Hallencreutz and Moyo, 51–113. Gweru: Mambo.
———. 1998. *Religion and Politics in Harare 1890–1980*. Uppsala: Swedish Institute of Missionary Research.
Hatfield, M. 1968. "How Can a Christian Be in Politics?" in *Protest and Politics: Christianity and Contemporary Affairs*, edited by R. G. Clouse et al. Greenwood: Attic.
Hirmer, O. 1982. *Marx-Money-Christ*. Gweru: Mambo.
Honor, T. 1956. *The Straight and Narrow Path*. London: Penguin.
Johanson, B. 2001. *Church and State in South Africa*. Braamfontein: The South African Council of Churches.

Bibliography

King, M. L. 1981. *Stride toward Freedom*. Queenstown: Edwin.

Kurewa, J. W. Z. 1997. *The Church in Mission: A Short History of the United Methodist Church in Zimbabwe, 1897–1997*. Nashville: Abingdon.

Lapsley, M. 1986. *Neutrality or Co-option: Anglican Church and State from 1964 until the Independence of Zimbabwe*. Gweru: Mambo.

———. 1988. "Anglican Church and State from UDI in 1965 until the Independence of Zimbabwe in 1980," in *Church and State in Zimbabwe*, edited by Hellencreutz and Moyo, 115–26. Gweru: Mambo.

Linden, I. 1980. *Church and State in Rhodesia, 1959–1979*. London: Longman.

Machoveč, M. 1976. *A Marxist Looks at Jesus*. London: Darton, Longman & Todd.

Martin, D., and P. Johnson. 1981. *The Struggle for Zimbabwe: The Chimurenga War*. Harare: Zimbabwe Publishing House.

McLaughlin, J. 1996. *On the Frontline: Catholic Missions in Zimbabwe's Liberation War*. Harare: Baobab.

Mkaronda, N. et al., eds. 2003. *Prophetic Witness in Zimbabwe: Critical Voices Emerging in Times of Crisis*. Harare: Ecumenical Support Services.

Mitchell, D. M. 1998. *In Search of Freedom: Josiah Chinamano*. Harare: Longman.

Munangagwa, E. D. 1989. "The Formation of the Zimbabwe People's Army: ZIPA," in *Turmoil and Tenacity*, edited by C. S. Banana, 143–46. Harare: College Press.

Mungazi, D. 1991. *The Honoured Crusade: Ralph Dodge's Theology of Liberation and Initiatives for Social Change in Zimbabwe*. Gweru: Mambo.

———. 2000. *In the Footsteps of The Masters: Desmond M. Tutu and Abel T. Muzorewa*. London: Westport.

Muzorewa, A. T. 1978. *Rise Up and Walk: Bishop Abel T. Muzorewa: An Autobiography*. Nashville: Abingdon.

Nkomo, J. M. 2001. *Nkomo: The Story of My Life*. Harare: SAPES Books.

Nyagumbo, M. 1980. *Some of Us Must Be With the People: An Autobiography from the Zimbabwe Struggle*. London: Allison and Busby.

Nyangoni, C., and G. Nyandoro, eds. 1979. *Zimbabwe Independent Movements: Selected Documents*. London: Rex Collins.

Pfeiffer, L. 1953. *Church, State, and Freedom*. Boston: Beacon.

Randolph, R .M. 1985. *Dawn in Zimbabwe: The Catholic Church in the New Order; A Report on the Activities of the Catholic Church in Zimbabwe for the Five Years, 1977–1981*. Gweru: Mambo.

Rauschenbusch, R. 1975. *Christianity and the Social Crisis*. London: SCM.

Shamuyarira, N. M. 1989. "An Overview of the Struggle for Unity and Independence," in *Turmoil and Tenacity*, edited by C. S. Banana, 13–24. Harare: College Press.

Sider, R. 1979. *Christ and Violence*. Herts: Lion.

Sithole, N. 1978. *In Justification of the Rhodesian Constitution Agreement*. Salisbury: Graham.

Smith, E. 1981. *The Ethics of Martin Luther King Jr*. Queenstown: Edwin.

Smith, D., C. Simpson, and I. Davies. 1981. *Mugabe*. Salisbury: Pioneer Head.

Smith, I. D. 1997. *Bitter Harvest: The Great Betrayal and the Dreadful Aftermath*. Johannesburg: Jonathan Ball.

Todd, J. 1972. *The Right to Say No*. London: Sidwich & Jackson.

Troeltsch, E. 1960. *The Social Teachings of the Christian Churches*. New York: Harper.

Walker, W. 1959. *A History of the Christian Church*. New York: Charles Scribner's Sons.

White, L. 2003. *The Assassination of Herbert Chitepo: Texts and Politics in Zimbabwe*. Indianapolis: Indiana University Press.

Other Documents, Journals, and Unpublished Works

All Africa Conference of Churches. *Drumbeats from Kampala*. London: Lutherworth, 1968.
Christian Council of Rhodesia Meetings Records, September 8, 1971; December 30, 1971; November 13, 1976.
Christian Council of Rhodesia Executive Committee Meetings Records, September 26, 1972; May 8, 1973; February 18, 1975; April 8, 1975.
Christian Council of Rhodesia Annual Meeting, April 1977.
Journal of Peacebuilding and Development: Critical Thinking and Constructive Action at the Intersection of Conflict, Development and Peace 1, no. 2 (2003).
Landmarks in Democracy: Developments in British Political History, April 1960.
Maenzanise, Beauty Roseberry. "Religion and Ritual in Zimbabwe: Quest for Liberation." Master of Sacred Theology thesis, Drew University.
Nyarota, Lloyd. "Christian Faith and Political Action." Diploma in Theology diss., United Theological College, Harare, Zimbabwe, 1995.
Official Journal of The United Methodist Church 1971, January 5, Mutambara.
Official Journal of The United Methodist Church 1972, January 4, Old Mutare.
Official Journal of The United Methodist Church 1973, January 8, St. Ignatius.
Social Principles of The United Methodist Church, 1997–2000.
Social Principles of The United Methodist Church, 2005–2008.
The Book of Discipline of The United Methodist Church, 1972.
The Book of Discipline of The United Methodist Church: Africa Central Conference Edition, 1990.
The Book of Discipline of The United Methodist Church, 2000.
"The Church and Human Relations," consultation held at The University College of Rhodesia and Nyasaland, August 25–29, 1965.
Umbowo editor's report, January–December 1976. Presented to the Christian Council Umbowo, October–November 1976.

Interviews

Bakare, Sebastian Bishop, Anglican Manicaland Diocesan Offices, April 27, 2005, Mutare.
Beta, Shadreck. TNT Headquarters, April 29, 2005, Mutare.
Chambara, Rev. Maxwell P., Mutare United Methodist Church District offices, April 29, 2005, Mutare.
De wolf, Rev. Shirley, Africa University, Institute of Peace Leadership and Governance, April 26, 2005, Mutare.
Former member of the Rhodesian Front Army, May 1, 2005, Chikanga, Mutare.
Jahwi, Davidson. Hilltop United Methodist Church, Sakubva, May 1, 2005, Mutare.
Kurewa, John W. Z. Professor, Africa University, Faculty of Theology, May 5, 2003, Mutare.
Mutume, Patrick Bishop, Catholic Bishop's residence Greenside, April 29, 2005, Mutare.
Muzarabani, Cde, ZNLWVA, Mutare offices, April 29, 2005, Mutare.

Bibliography

Muzorewa, Abel T. Bishop, Borrowdale home, April 28, 2005, Harare.
Sithole, Rev. Ndabaningi, Parliament of Zimbabwe, July 11, 1995, Harare.
Tekere, Edgar Borderville, April 4, 2005, Mutare.
Three members of the Zimbabwe National Liberation War Veterans Association, Mutare offices, April 29, 2005.
Two members of the Zimbabwe ex-detainees and restrictees association, May 1, 2005, Sakubva, Mutare.

www.ingramcontent.com/pod-product-compliance
Lightning Source LLC
Chambersburg PA
CBHW070522090426
42735CB00012B/2854